B'day May '03

Frisco / Katy

Color Guide to Freight Equipment

by Nicholas John Molo

Copyright © 2003
Morning Sun Books, Inc.

All rights reserved. This book may not be reproduced in part or in whole without written permission from the publisher, except in the case of brief quotations or reproductions of the cover for the purposes of review.

Library of Congress
Catalog Card No. 2002-114500

First Printing
ISBN 1-58248-110-5

Published by
Morning Sun Books, Inc.
9 Pheasant Lane
Scotch Plains, NJ 07076
Printed in Korea

Robert J. Yanosey, President
To access our full library *In Color* visit us at
www.morningsunbooks.com

Dedication

This book is dedicated to my wife, Caz, for her patience and encouragement throughout the lengthy process in completing this book. Thanks for your understanding through those many days and nights spent with "the book", it was worth it. Thanks Cazza! I would also like to thank my parents, Ray and Nick for introducing and nurturing my interests in trains since I was a "tack-a". I fondly remember many Sunday trips to "the port" passing railway lines and rail yards in my hometown of Adelaide, Australia. Love you all!

Acknowledgments

A book such as this one is the reflection of the efforts of many individuals. This includes the photographers, railroad researchers/historians and collectors of memorabilia that have provided freely their collections or knowledge of the FRISCO and/or The Katy. I think we are all fortunate to have so many foresighted photographers in our midst that "clicked" the photographs we see between these covers and beyond. I would like to extend my sincere thanks to the following contributors for all their efforts: Peter Arnold, Roger Bee, Craig Bossler, Steele Craver, Jim Eager, Paul Faulk, Ted Ferkenhoff, R. Fillman, Jim Gibson, Emery Gulash, Dan Holbrook, the late Pat Holden, Al Holtz, Jim Kinkaid, the late K.B. King Jr., Daniel Kohlberg, Ray Kucaba, Dick Kuelbs, Owen Leander, Tony Lovasz, Bill Phillips, Ron Plazzotta, Howard Robins, Jim Rogers, Lynn Savage, Allen Stanley, Roger Taylor, Eugene Van Dusen, Craig Walker, Paul Winters, Bernie Wooller, Richard Yaremko, Chuck Yungkurth (Rail Data Services), and Chuck Zeiler. Special thanks go out to Richard Yaremko and Bill Phillips for the full access to their collections of these great railroads. Their slides covered most of the key equipment in this book. Others provided further assistance which proved invaluable to the final product, including official equipment car diagrams and marketing materials, several editions of the *Official Railway Equipment Register*, and personal knowledge and memories. Thanks go to Allen Stanley, Jim Kinkaid, Roger Taylor, Mike Lutzenberger, Ted Ferkenhoff, Mike Condren, Doug Hughes and Dick Kuelbs. I would especially like to thank Jim Eager for encouraging me to start this project, his guidance and editing throughout the book and drawing on his immense knowledge. Finally, I would like to thank Bob Yanosey for his faith in the project and making it possible for all.

Nicholas Molo
August 2002

Table of Contents

Business Car 4	MKT Three-Bay Covered Hoppers 35	SLSF Flat Cars and Bulkhead Flats.......... 85
TEXAS SPECIAL Cars 5	MKT Airslide Covered Hoppers 38	SLSF Wood Racks........................... 88
MKT 40-Foot Boxcars........................ 8	MKT Autoracks.............................. 39	SLSF Equipped and Unequipped Gondolas.. 89
MKT 50-Foot Boxcars....................... 12	MKT Trailers and Tractors 41	SLSF Open Hoppers........................ 94
MKT 60-foot Boxcars....................... 18	MKT Non-Revenue Equipment 43	SLSF Woodchip Hoppers.................... 97
MKT 86-foot Boxcars....................... 20	MKT Cabooses.............................. 49	SLSF Two-Bay Covered Hoppers 98
MKT Stock Cars, Refrigerator Cars 21	SLSF 40-Foot Boxcars...................... 56	SLSF Three-Bay Covered Hoppers....... 101
MKT Insulated Boxcars..................... 22	SLSF 50-Foot Boxcars...................... 62	SLSF Airslide Covered Hoppers 105
MKT Flat Cars and Bulkhead Flats 25	SLSF 60-Foot Boxcars...................... 74	SLSF Autoracks............................ 107
MKT Equipped and Unequipped Gondolas... 29	SLSF 86-Foot Boxcars...................... 76	SLSF Tractors and Trailers 111
MKT Open Hoppers........................ 31	SLSF Stock Cars, Refrigerator Cars 77	SLSF Non-Revenue Equipment............ 113
MKT Two-Bay Covered Hoppers 33	SLSF Insulated Boxcars.................... 78	SLSF Cabooses........................... 121

(previous page) **MKT 5532, 5527, 5552, 5256;** The Katy had many boxcar types and in many paint schemes, but the most memorable and unmistakable were the extremely large billboard "M K T" cars either in the red and white or the later green and yellow. These cars were originally built in 1954 by Pullman-Standard as 97601-97800 (XM) and rebuilt by the Denison and Parsons Shops in 1971. The ever present Mr. Arnold was on hand in December 1972 at San Luis Obispo, California to capture this impressive string of MKT boxcars heading north to the Bay Area on the SP. The Katy had an ammunitions plant located on-line in McAlester, Oklahoma and had these cars assigned to the plant. The "AMMO" cars are probably heading toward the Sharpe Army Depot or Concord Naval Weapons Station. *(Peter Arnold)*

Frisco/Katy
Color Guide to Freight Equipment

Introduction

This book is a review of equipment that the Saint Louis – San Francisco Railway Company (Frisco) and Missouri-Kansas-Texas Railroad Company (The Katy) typically operated during the period when color photography was available. More information and history on both of these companies can also be found in these volumes of Morning Sun Books: *Frisco In Color* and *Missouri-Kansas-Texas Lines In Color*.

The Frisco had its beginnings in 1849 and was merged into the BN in November 1980. However, The Katy was chartered in 1865 and merged with the UP in August 1988. Both companies had unique emblems as corporate trademarks through most of their histories in one version or another. The Frisco coonskin was borne from a chance meeting during an inspection tour by Vice-President Nettleton with Neosho, MO agent Sam Albright, whom had caught and tanned "coon" hides on the depot for extra money. Mr. Nettleton purchased the hide and in 1896 the logo was developed, at first with the words "FRISCO LINE" placed inside the coonskin. The wording changed slightly another five times using "FRISCO SYSTEM" or "FRISCO LINES" or "FRISCO", one of these had the full title of the company within a ribbon below the coonskin. The coonskins shown within these pages were consistently used from 1947 and 1980, with only variations in size, the background color, or lack of background color or outline variations. MKT's emblem was not so unplanned it was designed by the Rand McNally Company and approved in 1889. The general shape was reminiscent of Spanish architectural elements found in the southwest particularly, The Alamo. Within the design were the company initials, at first "M-K-T" then "KATY". Below that lay a ribbon, which carried the official corporate name, which changed slightly through the years. The rule of thumb was when the company initials "M-K-T" were used, the ribbon had "MISSOURI-KANSAS-TEXAS LINES", when the "KATY" was used the "Lines" was dropped in the ribbon (this later variation is typically found throughout this book). Behind the ribbon lay a palm leaf that was a symbol of victory in the Indian Territory race in 1870. Only during President Deramus' era (1957-1961) did the overall emblem change considerably. When it was stretched horizontally, the background was changed to yellow and only "KATY" was placed within the emblem. Otherwise this emblem survived without major change until 1988, except for the use of yellow and green during the Whitman era.

Frisco's last passenger train was the KANSAS CITY-FLORIDA SPECIAL in November of 1967 and The Katy's last train THE TEXAS SPECIAL (by the end a Kansas City to Dallas run) ended in June of 1965. The joint SL-SF/M-K-T premier passenger operation, THE TEXAS SPECIAL, started in March of 1917 and prevailed till January 1959 providing nearly 43 years of service from St. Louis to San Antonio. One of the reasons to pair these rivals in a volume was the historical connection they had with THE TEXAS SPECIAL joint passenger service. Therefore, in this volume I have concentrated on typical passenger equipment found on this prestigious Midwest to Southwestern passenger train. The service was run on SL-SF from St. Louis, Missouri to Vinita, Oklahoma, then continuing on the MKT to the terminal of San Antonio, Texas. At its height THE TEXAS SPECIAL boasted through sleeper service with PRR to New York, Wabash to Chicago, and B&O to Washington, DC. The first regular service of a fully dieselized and streamlined consist for THE TEXAS SPECIAL was on May 15th, 1948. Luckily, the corporate color for both railroads was red and so was the significant color used on the joint equipment.

The purchase of freight car equipment reflected the traffic base of each company and their role in the greater nationwide transportation system. Through the years, the SL-SF consistently had more than twice the quantity of freight cars compared to the MKT. Although, their total route miles ranged within a thousand miles of each other. This explains why the greater proportion of the book is dedicated to the Frisco. For the most part, SL-SF and M-K-T utilized the same car types but the percentage between types varied. Due to Frisco serving many pulp and paper mills the use of wood racks and woodchip hoppers were the only types lacked by The Katy. Both leased many freight cars directly from builders or re-builders. However, The Katy was involved with a third party lease company, Bankers Leasing Corporation (a subsidiary of Southern Pacific) in 1965 to obtain new equipment. All of this leased equipment was conveniently marked with "BKTY" reporting marks. The MKT had shops in Denison, Parsons and Sedalia rebuilt and maintained many cars and built many unique cars. A specialty of the MKT shop forces was to reuse and recycle cars many times over in creative ways. The Frisco had several shops located around the system. In the late sixties, they consolidated all of them in Springfield, Missouri and were known as the Consolidated Mechanical Shops (CMS) or simply the Springfield shops. They performed many rebuildings and reconditioning of equipment, averaging 500 cars per year between 1971 and 1975. In the late seventies, CMS built thousands of new cars in a single assembly line, while still rebuilding cars on three other lines. The new car types included 100-ton hoppers, 100-ton covered hoppers, cabooses, and even fully enclosed autoracks.

The book is organized in the following manner: the equipment is presented from the earliest to latest acquisition dates, with respect to leased equipment I have used the start date of the lease (which coincided with the built or rebuilt dates). Generally, the Frisco and The Katy did not use a systemic alpha or numeric classification system. However, I have listed their number series, tons, AAR car code, lengths and cubic capacity wherever applicable. The exceptions were the "BKTY" marked cars that used a SP alphanumeric classification system, even though one group of these cars did not receive that designation. It was impossible to cover all variations and equipment in this volume. So, the most typical equipment is represented with the more typical paint scheme, if the slides were available. Whenever possible the detailed captions capture the pertinent information about the history and purpose of each piece of equipment. I trust you will enjoy these colorful railroads as much as I have enjoyed researching and writing about them. I know that the following images will allow us to capture the spirit of The Katy and Frisco fleets forever.

FRISCO Passenger Equipment M·K·T

Business Cars

MKT 403; series 400-404; Business Car; 71'8" IL

▶ A step into the past, in September 1990, number 403 is resplendent in Atlanta, Georgia. This all steel Business Car was purchased by Dr. and Mrs. Marshall and they have completely restored the car to its original state. This includes the MKT drumhead, Pullman green exterior paint and Dulux gold lettering and interior details like a JennAir kitchen stove, red leather upholstery, brass grille work around the baseboard heaters and a full set of silverware. *(Howard L. Robins)*

MKT 1046; *Lewa;* **Business Car; 71'8" IL**

◀ The *Lewa* Business Car was originally a Diner (probably ACF) rebuilt by the MKT Sedalia Shops in 1948 as number 403 in Pullman green. The *Lewa* is captured near Dallas Union Terminal in May 1980 in a version of Whitman Green. It seems that current MKT President Reginald N. Whitman has continued some traditions from his predecessor John Barriger III, by having the premier Business car stationed on the Dallas Union Terminal tracks.

(Tony Lovasz)

SLSF *Missouri;* **Business Car 75'1" IL**

▶ The *Missouri* started life as a 1912 ACF-built all steel construction Coach, converted to a Diner and eventually a Business Car. The Frisco Springfield Shops in all cases carried out the conversions. Howard snapped a highly polished and double pin stripped *Missouri*, being attached to a northbound train in Birmingham, AL in 1956. Sometime between 1962 and 1964 it was numbered to *#1* and its air-conditioning was updated from an ice system to a Waukesha. It was remodeled by BN in 1985 and is now called *Meramec River (BNA9)*. The Meramec River runs southwest from St. Louis Missouri, a subtle reminder of its Frisco heritage. *(Howard L. Robins)*

Texas Special Cars

KATY 434; *Muskogee*; **series 434, 436, 437, 439;**
Heavyweight Diner-Lounge car; 78'1" IL

▶ The Katy and Frisco in 1947 each received one set of Pullman-Standard lightweight streamline trains for the joint TEXAS SPECIAL passenger service. The service was between St. Louis and San Antonio; at the latter location the MKT did not have sufficient time to turn the train for the return trip. So therefore, both companies had to make up a third trainset out of heavyweight equipment painted in red and silver. Here is an example of one of these repainted heavyweights *Muskogee*, a Diner-Lounge car built by ACF in 1931, on Grand Trunk Western track in South Bend, Indiana on October the 13th 1951. Note that the trim is a shadow striping silver paint to mimic stainless steel fluting of the lightweight cars. Not until a 1955 re-order of lightweight cars was there any relief for these heavyweight cars, although in-sufficient head-end and observation cars still prevailed. *Muskogee* was able to dine 24 persons and seat an additional 14 persons in the lounge section. *(Eugene Van Dusen)*

FRISCO 1250; *Olivette*; **series KATY 1200-1201, FRISCO**
1250-1258; Coach car; 78'5" IL

▲ From the original Pullman-Standard order of 1947, the *Olivette* was built at the Chicago plant in November of that year. The car was named after Olivette, Missouri, a small town just west of St. Louis. All the Frisco Coach cars were named after small towns around St. Louis. The majority of these cars were constructed in Corten steel, with exterior corrugated stainless steel trim and some aluminum trim for the interior. They originally came equipped with Carrier Steam Ejector air-conditioning. The Olivette has seen better days as it languishes on the Springfield Shop tracks on May 16, 1970. The original roof color for THE TEXAS SPECIAL cars was red, so the 1250 has had its roof repainted to black, which a few cars did receive later. *(Owen Leander)*

FRISCO 1259; *Picardy Lane*; **series KATY 1202R-1207,**
FRISCO 1259; Coach car; 78'5" IL

▲ *Picardy Lane* was one of the additional coach cars ordered by the SLSF and MKT with Pullman-Standard in 1955 to create a third trainset for THE TEXAS SPECIAL. The other 1955 Chair cars (as MKT called them) were KATY 1203-1207; *Garland*, *Pryor*, *New Braunfels*, *McAlester*, and *Denton* respectively and a Combination Chair-Lounge-Buffet car KATY 1301 named *Temple*, all MKT cars were named after on-line towns. A replacement Chair car purchased in 1954, 1202R, *J.Pinckney Henderson* was the Pullman-Standard ex-stainless steel demonstrator car. Paul Winters was lucky enough to obtain an in-service photograph of *Picardy Lane* west of 21st Street in St. Louis in February 1963. In 1963 THE TEXAS SPECIAL did not exist as a joint service with the MKT and SLSF, it prevailed until January 4th 1959. THE TEXAS SPECIAL boasted through sleeper service from New York (PRR), Chicago (Wabash) and Washington (B&O) to Texas destinations. The Frisco continued these connections since we can see Pullmans from the Pennsy and Wabash *Clover Plateau* on either side of *Picardy Lane*. *(Paul C. Winters)*

FRISCO 1456; *Eugene Field*; **series 1450-1466; Sleeper; 78'5" IL**

▶ The first car behind the CB&Q E-units on this troop train is Sleeper *Eugene Field* a Pullman-Standard product from the original 1948 order. Eugene Field is a renowned Missouri children's poet. The names in the Frisco series up to #1456 were of other famous Missourians. The Katy cars were named after famous persons in the historical development of Texas. This troop train is heading for Union Station on the Burlington Route passing the Pennsylvania Railroad Polk Street Freight Station in Chicago, Illinois on an August day in 1966. This elevated view allows a good view of the clean rooflines with minimal details on these Pullmans. *Eugene Field* was sold to the Nord Company and rebuilt as a Photo Instruction car, and later sold to a collector in the East.
(Ronald A. Plazzotta)

FRISCO 1463; *Canadian River*; **series 1450-1466; Sleeper; 78'5" IL**

▼ Both Frisco sleepers are in view on the same troop train in Chicago, Illinois 1966, second in the consist is the *Canadian River* another Pullman-Standard product from the original 1948 order. The second half of the Frisco sleeper series was named after rivers that the Frisco crosses on its system. This series of cars had four bedrooms with private toilets and fourteen roomettes. This view also allows us to see how extensive the operations were at the Pennsylvania Railroad Polk Street Freight Station in Chicago in 1966. *(Ronald A. Plazzotta)*

KATY 1502; *William B. Travis*; **series 1500-1506; Sleeper; 78'4" IL**

▼ As per the Frisco cars these sleepers had four bedrooms and fourteen roomettes and came from the original 1948 Pullman-Standard order. The Katy cars were named after famous persons in the historical development of Texas. Number 1502 was named in honor of William B. Travis, the famous Texas commander at the Battle of the Alamo where he lost his life at age 26 in 1836. These cars came equipped with Safety Carrier steam ejector air-conditioning. Bill Phillips found and shot fluted stainless steel 1502 at Denison Texas in April 1969, along with other passenger cars on the condemned line. Passenger service on the MKT ended four years earlier on 30 June 1965.
(Bill Phillips)

KATY 1506; *Amon B. King*; **series 1500-1506; Sleeper; 78'4" IL**
▲ The last in the Katy series of sleepers, number 1506 was named in honor of Amon B. King, a famous captain at the Battle of Refugio. Like the others in the series it was built by Pullman-Standard in 1948. These cars came equipped with Safety Carrier steam ejector air-conditioning. Howard captured the *Amon B. King* close to home in Atlanta, Georgia in June 1968, along with other sleepers: a Frisco twin and a Union Pacific one to the right.
(Howard L. Robins)

FRISCO 1550; *Tulsa*; **series 1550-1551; Diner-Lounge-Observation car; 81'11" IL**
▲ *Tulsa* again came from the original Pullman-Standard order, the other being *Oklahoma City*, both being built in May of 1948 and appointed for dining 28 persons and seating for 17 in the observation section of the car. The three smaller windows to the rear of the car mark the location of the kitchen. The Katy did not purchase any equivalent cars, they instead required two Combination-Chair-Lounge-Buffet cars numbered and named 1300 *Mirabeau B. Lamar* (built 1948) and 1301 *Temple* (built in 1955). These cars came equipped with Safety Carrier steam ejector and Electro-Mechanical air-conditioning respectively. Northwest Oklahoma Railroad purchased number 1550 *Tulsa* in the seventies, where it is found on that railroad at Woodward, Oklahoma in June the 27th 1974. The Frisco later did paint a small number of their passenger cars black replacing the red. *(Peter Arnold collection)*

KATY 1400; *Stephen F. Austin*; **series KATY 1400, FRISCO 1350; Observation car; 78'5" IL**
▶ Built in 1948 by Pullman-Standard as part of the original THE TEXAS SPECIAL train set. Both railroads only had one Observation car each, the Frisco's was 1350 the *Joseph Pulitzer*. They were designed with two bedrooms and a single luxurious drawing room. Number 1400 was named in honor of Stephen F. Austin, considered the founder of Anglo-American Texas. These cars came equipped with Safety Carrier steam ejector air-conditioning. Faded paint and without its drumhead logo in an unknown location on a day in August 1963.
(Owen Leander collection)

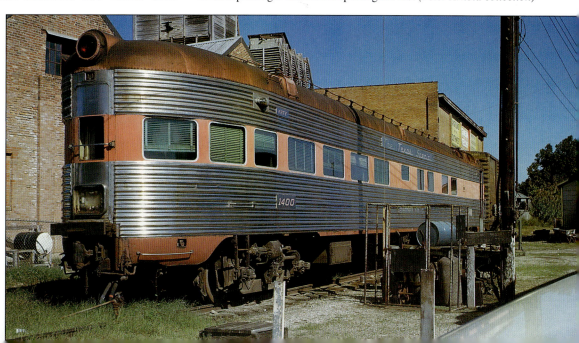

M·K·T Equipped and Unequipped Boxcars

40-Foot Boxcars

MKT 79112; series 79001-79157
40-ton XM; 40'6" IL; 3849 cu. ft.

▼ This car started out life as a refrigerator car built in 1923 by General American Car Co. as series 52001-52200. It was converted by the MKT Denison, Texas shops in 1943, where the cars received a Stanray riveted roof and 6'0" Youngstown doors with Camel door fixtures amongst other "modern" improvements. The Katy usually numbered their cars starting with a number "1" instead of "0" right up to the mid-fifties. The classic Sloan yellow paint scheme was applied during the rebuilding, it's hard to see much of the yellow color on this badly faded and peeled car. It was captured at Ray Yard, Denison in October 1978 in maintenance of way service, note the small "MWM" stenciling to the lower right.

(Rail Data Services)

MKT 95954; series 95000-95999
50-ton XM; 40'6" IL; 3128 cu. ft.

▶ The Katy approached Mount Vernon Car Co. to build 1000 general service boxcars to be completed in 1925. The first 500 cars received Camel No. 32 doors and the last came with National Bottom Hung doors. Both series had Hutchins Dry Lading roofs and vertical Universal hand brakes. The 95954 has been recently re-weighed at Ray Yard in June 1964 and the car number re-stenciled. Noted railroad photographer Bernie Wooller photographed it three months later, probably close to home in Huntsville, Alabama. The car appears in the typical paint scheme when built a very simple boxcar red and the "M – K – T " hyphenated for reporting marks. *(Bernie Wooller)*

MKT 45360; series 45001-45385
◀ **40-ton XMR; 40'6" IL; 3978 cu. ft.**

In 1946, President Matthew Sloan initiated the company slogan "The Katy – Serves the Southwest Well". Shown is one of the first examples of this slogan being applied to a MKT Automobile car. Denison Shop forces built 385 cars in 1945 and 1946 from Youngstown steel body parts and 7'0" and 8'0" corrugated sliding doors with Murphy steel roofs. Other equipment applied were Evans 12-F auto racks (signified by the white stripe on the right door and "12-F " stenciling), Universal W 2000 hand brakes with Miner draft gear. A majority of these cars were rebuilt by MKT in 1962 and again in 1965 and renumbered 2400-2599 and 2600-2749 respectively. Number 45260 sits untouched on a Dallas siding in February 1973. *(Steele Craver)*

MKT 5532; series 5500-5599
55-ton XL; 40'6" IL; 3901 cu. ft.; ASSIGNED MCALESTER OKLA. FOR AMMO. LOADING

▲ In November and December 1954 Pullman-Standard's Bessemer plant built forty and fifty-foot PS-1 design boxcars for MKT. Numbers 97601 to 97800 were the forty-footers and numbers 99201 to 99500 were the fifty-footers. Between July and December 1971 the MKT Parsons, Kansas and Denison, Texas shops rebuilt at least 98 of the 200 forty-foot cars with 6'0" Youngstown doors and wood floors. These cars were incorrectly classified "XL", equipped boxcars, but assigned for loading at an ammunitions plant in McAlester, Oklahoma. Here we see 5532 heading north loaded (note the tack board placards and compressed truck springs) through San Luis Obispo, CA on the SP in 1973 to US Naval and Army storage facilities in northern California. Its been speculated that MKT specifically developed the extra large "M K T" paint scheme to alert all railroads of their dangerous load from great distances. The original solid bearing trucks have been wisely retrofitted with roller bearings. *(Peter Arnold)*

MKT 92463; series 92301-92650
55-ton XM; 40'6" IL; 3895 cu. ft.

▼ ACF's St. Louis plant built 350 boxcars between September and December of 1956 boxcars. One of the cars in the series is still in great condition in its as-delivered paint scheme when it was recorded in 1968, except for a re-weigh date and station initials of SS-6-65. The 1946 slogan updated to "The Katy SERVING THE GREAT SOUTHWEST", the "GREAT" being added for a very short time on ACF cars purchased in 1956. This series of cars was delivered with 6'0" Youngstown doors, lading band anchors (symbol painted on the door) and 20'8" centered nailable steel floors (stenciled to the left of the door). *(Rail Data Services)*

**MKT 92366; series 92349, 92366, 92445, 92619, 92630
55-ton XP or XL; 40'6" IL; 3895 cu. ft.;
FLOUR LOADING ONLY
WHEN EMPTY RETURN TO AGENT TRRA
CARRIE AVENUE YARD ST. LOUIS, MO.**

▶ The above numbered cars were dedicated to Flour Loading Only on the TRRA in north St. Louis. The TRRA served Continental Baking Co. (Ralston Purina), Valier Spies Mill and Pillsbury flourmills. The five cars were randomly selected from the 1956 ACF built 92301-92650 boxcars and upgraded by the Denison shops in July 1971. The interiors received food grade paint, roof walks were removed and they were either classified as XP or XL boxcars. The car body was painted a green, this is not the Whitman green commencing in 1971, but a slightly darker shade. A white stripe and lettering (not yellow) finished the paint scheme to identify the special assignment of these cars. Photographed in October 1979. *(Steele Craver)*

**MKT 9037; series 9036-9049, 9075
55-ton XME; 40'11" IL; 3990 cu. ft.
WHEN EMPTY RETURN TO
AGENT L&N LOUISVILLE KY.**

◀ A small order from Thrall Car Co. arrived in February 1960 originally numbered 36 to 49 and 75. Specifically purchased for the GE appliance pool, the series received large 8'0" Superior sliding doors. Numbers 36, 37, 38 came equipped with 19-Belt Evans DF-2 loaders while the others had 9-Belt Evans DF-2 utility loaders. Note the yellow "DF" on the right side and small stencil "DF EQUIPPED" near the numbers. Number 9037 was slightly upgraded (note the gussets at the lower door openings), reweighed and repainted in Whitman green and yellow at Denison in August of 1974. Steele captured 9037 and twin 9075 in red in Dallas on a March day in 1976. The quirky off-series numbering of 75 was to avoid a 1959 Thrall order of bulkhead flatcars in series 50 to 74.

(Steele Craver)

**MKT 941; series 940-948 50-ton XML;
40'6" IL; 3955 cu. ft.
WHEN EMPTY
RETURN TO AGENT,
P.R.R., COLUMBUS,
OHIO.**

▶ These Pullman-Standard cars were built in July 1961 with the Deramus simplified and extended "KATY" emblem of 1956. Specifically purchased for appliance service for either Westinghouse Electric or Whirlpool, the series received larger 9'0" P-S six panel sliding doors and 9-Belt Evans DF-2 loaders. Found in the receiving tracks of Yard B in the assigned city on the 29th of July 1962.

(Paul C. Winters)

MKT 6771; series 6700-6899 55-ton XM; 40'6" IL; 3898 cu. ft.

◀ In 1965 President Barriger set out to improve Katy's freight service and equipment, he also re-introduced the traditional 1889 emblem with "KATY" instead of "M-K-T". Part of this $10 million improvement plan was to sell existing forty-foot cars, have them modernized and lease them back. The cars came from Pressed Steel Car Co., American Car and Foundry and Pullman-Standard built between 1948 and 1953, number 6771 originally from Pressed Steel built in January 1949 is captured in Fort Worth on the 27th of September 1981. United States Railway Equipment Co. was the re-conditioner and lessor from their Washington, Indiana plant in April 1967. *(Richard Yaremko)*

MKT 5101; series 5100-5199 55-ton XM and XP; 40'6" IL; 3978 cu. ft.

▼ Built between April and May 1968 by the ACF St. Louis plant, delivered with a 6 foot Youngstown corrugated sliding door and Precision Design pressed panels. To the author's knowledge these were the only examples of "Precision" pressed panels constructed on a forty-foot boxcar. Found in great condition in Fort Worth on the 7th of September 1981 with a re-weigh from Muskogee 8.75 with some classic but subtle graffiti. Fifteen cars from this series had their interiors painted and were assigned for flour loading, therefore the XP classification. *(Ronald A. Plazzotta)*

50-Foot Boxcars

MKT 99150; series 99001-99200
55-ton XM; 50'6" IL; 4861 cu. ft.
▲ The MKT received these 4861 cubic foot ACF St. Louis-built general-purpose boxcars between April and June of 1953. The cars received riveted side panels and 8'0" Superior 6 panel sliding doors. Richard captured 99150 in Dallas on October the 22nd 1983 with the majority of its original paint scheme intact. Especially notice the 20'8" nailable steel floor center of car stencil. Some of these cars were sold and modernized by United States Railway Equipment Co. then leased back to MKT in 1970. *(Richard Yaremko)*

MKT 99263; series 99201-99500
55-ton XM; 50'6" IL; 4864 cu. ft.
▼ The MKT ordered the Pullman-Standard 4864 cubic foot boxcar the following year, constructed at the Bessemer plant in November to December 1954. Even though these cars had very similar cubic capacity as the 1953 ACF cars they differed greatly. They were built with welded side panels, had 7'0" and 8'0" Youngstown sliding doors and centered 24' nailable steel floor. Number 99263 is along way from home in San Francisco, California on November 3, 1964. *(Rail Data Services)*

MKT 2330; series 2300-2343
55-ton XM; 50'6" IL; 4864 cu. ft.
▲ Photographed on July 18 1979 in Dolton, Illinois in Whitman green and very large yellow "M K T" reminiscent of the "AMMO" cars. The Katy tried to out-do all the competitor car billboards. This series were rebuilt by the Denison shops from March to May 1975 from 1955 Pullman-Standard 4790 cu. ft. XL series 90101-90150. The rebuilding included the removal of the 9-Belt Evans DF-2 loaders and roof walks, therefore the larger cubic capacity. The 8'0" Superior sliding doors and openings were reinforced with riveted and welded gussets and stiffened side sill. *(Raymond F. Kucaba)*

MKT 90183; series 90151-90200
55-ton XML; 50'6" IL; 4879 cu. ft.
▼ American Foundry and Car Company's St. Louis plant built these equipped boxcars in October 1956. By the time, Dan found 90183 in Pasco, Washington in May 1974, had its assignment note painted out and maybe lost its Evans DF Utility Loaders. This series of cars had the "…GREAT SOUTHWEST" paint scheme applied in 1956; additionally it received a unique DF MKT emblem. Welded side panels, 8'0" Youngstown sliding doors and the center of car 24' nailable steel flooring came standard. *(Dan Holbrook)*

MKT 99712; series 9965199800 55-ton XM and XML (later XL); 50'6" IL; 4950 cu. ft. WHEN EMPTY RETURN TO AGENT, G.T.W. R.R., WATERFORD, MICH.

◀ The yellow "DF" to the upper right stands for Damage-Free equipped, eight cars from this series had 19 Belt Evans DF Utility Loaders for Buick Auto Parts loading on the Grand Trunk. American Car and Foundry Company's St. Louis plant built these boxcars in the third quarter of 1956. All cars had 7' and 8' offset Youngstown sliding doors and the centers of car have 24' nailable steel flooring. In August the 11th 1979 number 99712 was captured at Blue Island, Illinois in a rusted and faded red paint with Deramus extended Katy emblem. *(Raymond F. Kucaba)*

MKT 2214; series 2200-2299 55-ton XM; 50'6" IL; 4937 cu. ft.

▶ MKT Parsons shops in 1972 rebuilt cars from boxcars from the series 99651-99800 ACF built in 1956. Part of the rebuilding program was to remove roof walks, accordingly cutting down the ladders and strengthen the door openings with gussets. The cars retained their 7' and 8' offset Youngstown sliding doors and the centers of car have 24' nailable steel flooring. The standard paint scheme in 1972 called for Whitman green with 30" high yellow "MKT" letters, shown in Las Vegas, Nevada May 18, 1977. *(Peter Arnold)*

MKT 1441; series 1400-1449 77-ton XL; 50'6" IL; 4952 cu. ft. WHEN EMPTY RETURN TO AGENT, P.R.R., LANSING, ILLINOIS

▼ Here is one of the billboarded HYDROFRAME-60 cushioned underframe 77-ton cars that were built at Pullman-Standard's Michigan City plant in April 1964. These cars came equipped with either single or 9 belt Evans DF-2 Loaders, some of which were removed by 1980 and re-classed XM. Nine cars of the series (9 Beltequipped) like the example shown were assigned to Bomb Casings loading on the Pennsy in Illinois. The loads probably were off-loaded at the ammunition plant in McAlester, Oklahoma. Even by the date of the shot on September 6th 1982 in Fort Worth, 1441 retains its roof walks, high ladders, full length nailable steel flooring, 9'0" P-S 6 panel sliding door and original Deramus paint scheme. *(Bill Phillips)*

BKTY 20572; series 20500-20641; class B-70-34
78-ton XM; 50'6" IL; 4926 cu. ft.

▲ Barriger's commitment to improved freight service meant new cars for shippers and the Katy responded by leasing new cars instead of purchasing them. The cars that were leased for 15 years had BKTY reporting marks, the "B" standing for Bankers Leasing Corporation, a Southern Pacific affiliate and the property of The Commonwealth Plan Inc. These ACF built cars ordered for June to August 1966 followed the SP system of class designation Boxcar-70-ton-34th series. These 142 cars and an order of 50 flatcars were for general service, unlike most other specially equipped BKTY cars. Bill's low angle shot clearly shows the silhouette of the distinctive SP-favored HYDRA-CUSHION cylinder and the 10'0" Youngstown plug doors. Dallas, Texas February 21 1982.
(Bill Phillips)

MKT 11575; series 11400-11749;
class B-70-33 77-ton XM; 50'6" IL; 4980 cu. ft.

▼ HYDRA-CUSHION underframes and centered 7-foot plus 8-foot Superior 6-panel sliding doors were featured on this 350-car order. Katy received this group from Evans Products between March and September 1967. Ironically this order was stenciled with an SP class designation of B-70-33, even though these were not BKTY leased cars. Perhaps they were to supplement the SP Pacific Northwest lumber service. Note the "UNLOAD FROM THIS SIDE" placard on the door tack board and steel banding across the doors. Parsons, Kansas August 14, 1977. *(Richard Yaremko)*

MKT 11821; series 11750-11874; class B-70-33
75-ton XL; 50'6" IL; 4980 cu. ft.

▲ A follow-up 125-car order from Evans arrived in March to September 1967, equipped with Evans one-piece movable bulkheads, HYDRA-CUSHION underframe and 10-foot Superior plug doors. Again this order arrived stenciled with an SP class designation of B-70-33, although these were not leased cars. The assignment had been painted-out and the car may have lost its DF-Bulkheads when it was re-weighed at Raytown Yard in Denison in September 1977. Number 11821 was found at the same location on the 30th of November 1980. MKT operated them as quoted in their marketing material, "Used for miscellaneous manufactured products not requiring protection against extreme temperatures."

(Richard Yaremko)

MKT 11997; series 11875-11992, 11993-11999;
class B-70-33 76.5-ton XL; 50'6" IL; 4980, 4900 cu. ft.
WHEN EMPTY RETURN VIA REVERSE ROUTE TO NYC AGENT MORAINE, OHIO

▼ Mr. Wooller captured an almost new car in Huntsville, Alabama, while on the L&N or Southern. This follow-up order with Evans arrived in October 1967, however these came with 10-foot Superior 6-panel sliding doors. The last seven cars had 4900 cubic foot capacity, probably reduced due to auto parts pallets for the GM plant in Moraine.

(Bernie Wooller)

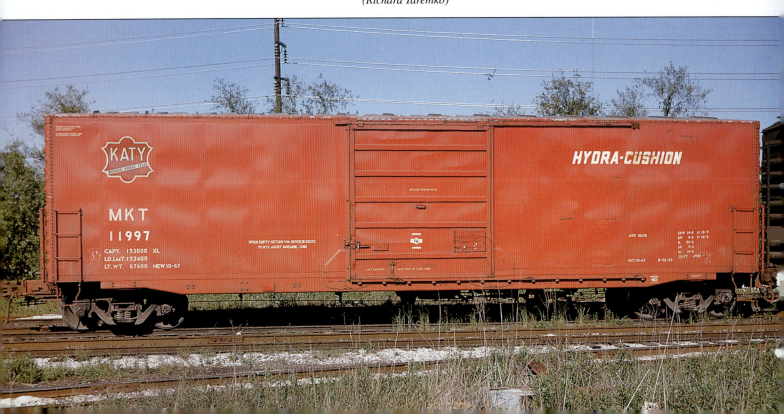

MKT 1976; series 1900-2199
77-ton XM; 50'6" IL; 4950 cu. ft.
▲ There is no mistaking this car is an ACF product with the applied ACF-FREIGHT-SAVER CUSHIONED logo. This example also clearly shows the ACF Precision Design pressed panels to the right of the 10'0" Youngstown corrugated sliding door. Built at the St. Louis plant in June of 1968, it demonstrates the Barriger red KATY emblem paint scheme on a hot afternoon of August 14th 1977 in Parsons, Kansas. *(Richard Yaremko)*

BKTY 18356; series 18000-18499
70-ton XL; 50'6" IL; 4957 cu. ft.
▼ A slight variation on the Barriger's paint scheme was the addition of the black ends, shown in exquisite condition at two months old on April 11, 1970. It was one of the few series of BKTY cars not having a SP class designation stenciled on. Built at the Pullman-Standard Bessemer shops with belt rail loaders, P-S corrugated sliding doors, low brake wheels and ladders and without roof walks. *(Craig T. Bossler)*

60-Foot Boxcars

MKT 8644; series 8600-8699; class B-70-33
70.5-ton XL; 60'9" IL; 6450 cu. ft.

▶ Ray Kucaba found number 8644 in Kansas City, Kansas on September 30th 1984 with its door open showing some of the nine belt rails that equipped these cars. The end clearly shows coupler extension details, original low ladders, low-mounted AJAX handbrake and the slight peak of the galvanized roof. This group of 60-foot Evans Products cars were built between March and September 1967. They were purchased mainly for auto parts traffic, probably for Ford and General Motors which were major customers for MKT. Besides the Evans belt rails the cars had a HYDRA-CUSHION TYPE 20-14 underframe and 10-foot Superior seven panel sliding doors. They received the SP class designation of B-70-33, although they were not BKTY cars.
(Raymond F. Kucaba)

MKT 8785; series 8700-8799; class B-70-33
70.5-ton XML; 60'9" IL; 6450 cu. ft.

▼ These 60-foot Evans Products cars built in March and April 1967, preceded the 50-foot version (MKT 11750-11874) by four months. The cars were similarly equipped with Evans one-piece movable DF-Bulkheads, HYDRA-CUSHION underframe and 10-foot Superior plug doors, although 10" taller. These were not leased cars, however they still received the stenciled SP class B-70-33. The Katy initially used these cars for miscellaneous manufactured products that did not requiring protection against extreme temperatures but 8785 is loaded with corrosive materials on this April 1980 day in Fort Worth. The DF bulkheads will stop any shifting in transit for this dangerous load!
(Bill Phillips)

MKT 8511; series 8510-8511
MKT 8528; series 8520-8534
70-ton XL; 60'9" IL; 6330 cu. ft. WHEN EMPTY RETURN TO AGENT B&O R.R. MARTINSBURG W.VA.

▲▼ These two groups of cars were purchased for auto parts traffic and our two examples both have an assignment to Martinsburg West Virginia. This was the location of an auto parts warehouse for General Motors on the B&O. The cars were built in September 1968 by ACF with *FREIGHT-SAVER* CUSHIONED underframes, nine belt rails from Evans, and PRECISION DESIGN strengthening ribs to the opening side of the doors. The first series of cars received ten-foot Youngstown corrugated sliding doors and the second series came with two eight-foot doors per side. *(both, Ronald A. Plazzotta)*

MKT 8024; series 8000-8050
83-ton XP; 60'9" IL; 6311 cu. ft.;
CODE 2198 WHEN EMPTY RETURN TO MKT AGENT BROKEN ARROW, OKLA.

▶ These 83-ton cars arrived in Whitman green when new in February 1979 from Fruit Growers Express' plant in Alexandria, Virginia. This is what is meant by "FULLY LOADED", 11 belt rails, 2 bulkheads, load dividers, nailable steel floor (entire car length), Freightmaster 15 inch travel end-of-car cushioning, and pairs of 8'0" Youngstown exterior post plug doors. These cars participated in the Ford glass pool. Central Oklahoma is a large silica mining area, so it is no wonder that glass is manufactured in Broken Arrow, OK near Tulsa. This XP Plate E car was photographed on March 8th 1984 in Parsons, Kansas. *(Ronald A. Plazzotta)*

86-foot Boxcars

MKT 8500, 8501; series 8500-8504
100-ton XML; 86'6" IL; 10000 cu. ft.
WHEN EMPTY RETURN TO
WABASH R.R., BUFFALO, N.Y.

▲ ▶ Two months old in November 1964 and sporting a spotless Deramus era paint scheme with shiny 10-foot aluminum plug doors. These immense cars were built specifically for auto stampings; number 8500 was assigned to a Ford stamping plant pool in Buffalo, NY on the Wabash. These 100-ton 10000 cubic foot hi-cube cars were built by Greenville and had a cushioned underframe, highlighted in yellow with relatively small letters. When number 8501 was repainted in green in 1978, it didn't retain its assignment stencil but it probably was still in Ford service when caught on October 26th 1983.
(Emery J. Gulash and Pat Holden, Jim Eager collection)

MKT 8541; series 8541-8549
100-ton XL; 86'6" IL; 10000 cu. ft.

▼ By the time this group of cars was received in January 1969, Katy president Deramus was out and replaced by Barriger. Even though the general car color stayed red, the use of KATY and MKT in yellow emphasized president Barriger's touch. Built specifically for auto stampings, this particular car is probably assigned to a Ford stamping plant pool but the assignment is not legible. The Katy stayed with Greenville and cushioned underframes for all their 86-foot cars. San Luis Obispo, California December 1971. *(Peter Arnold)*

Stock Cars

Refrigerator Cars

**MKT 4667, 4703, 47056, 4714;
series 4600-4899 and 47001-47500
40-ton SM; 40'6" IL; 2980 cu. ft.**

▲ This distant photo was the only one the publisher was able to find, although it was worthy enough to include for more than just the string of Katy stock cars. Mr. Winters found and photographed this scene in May 1965. The second series was built by MKT in 1937. The first series were painted black and had smooth steel sheets for their roofs, whilst number 47056 was painted in the Sloan yellow paint scheme of 1943-1945 both cars had six-foot sliding doors. Up to 295 cars from the 4600 to 4899 series were still present on the MKT roster up to late 1967. *(Paul C. Winters)*

**BKTY 19; series 1-50
66-ton RPL; 50'9" IL; 4022 cu. ft.**

▼ This is the only group of mechanical reefers the Katy purchased or leased; they were delivered in March 1966 from Pacific Car and Foundry. A Southern Pacific subsidiary, the Bankers Leasing Corporation purchased all the "BKTY" cars care of The Commonwealth Plan Inc. and leased them to MKT for 15 years. The remittances and per diem reports were sent initially to Boston, MA and later to San Mateo, CA. The cars were typically equipped with HYDRA-CUSHION underframes (with SP influence), 2-piece Unarco load dividers and nine-foot Youngstown plug doors. Katy listed the following possible loads in their literature: frozen foodstuffs, such as poultry, packing house products, fruits and vegetables and fruit juices, also for non-frozen foodstuffs requiring refrigeration like shortening, candy, dough, other bakery goods, margarine, salad dressing and dairy products. Bill recorded number 19 broadside in Dallas in October 1977, easily showing the HYDRA-CUSHION cylinder, diesel tanks for the refrigeration unit, and white roof and roof walk. *(Bill Phillips)*

Insulated Boxcars

**GARX 50833;
series 50800-50850
48-ton RBL; 50'1" IL;
4360 cu. ft.**

▶ The first RBL's the Katy operated were built and leased by General American Car Co. in 1955. Mr. King thankfully captured this classic fifties-era General American/Katy with black ends and yellow paint scheme in the built year. Notice that the 7'7" Youngstown plug door has a small bar and ball symbol with the DF-2 logo within to signify that the car has Evans DF-2 belt rails equipment. One can speculate that General American wanted to make their slogan NO DAMAGE to be more noticeable than the Evans DF logo. A REA trailer stands on the ready near the car.
(K. B. King Jr.,
Richard Yaremko collection)

**MKT 921; series 917-923
77-ton RBL; 50'1" IL; 4604 cu. ft.**

◀ The Katy classed these insulated cars as "Grocery Cars" to carry products like beer and canned goods; North American Car Co. built them in January 1964. Remarkably, the original Deramus paint scheme has lasted very well after fifteen years in this April 1979 Fort Worth photo. The 10-foot Superior plug doors allowed easier access for forklift loading compared to the previous example. The Evans DF-B equipment and cushioned underframe all help to secure and safely transport the high valued lading.
(Bill Phillips)

**BKTY 88; series 75-99;
class B-100-8
90-ton RBL; 50'2" IL;
5050 cu. ft.
RETURN WHEN EMPTY TO
AGENT M D & W RY**

▶ Once the MKT realized the profitability and the customer need for RBL's, it was an easy decision to lease more, like this group of 25 cars built by PCF in February 1966. The ever present and "BIG" Katy fan Bill Phillips shot this car not far from home in Dallas exactly sixteen years after its built date. Note the SP class B-100-8, the SP-preferred HYDRA-CUSHION underframe, and Car-Pac internal load protection devices include: 9-belt rails, 22-crossmembers, 16-deckboards and 8-doorbars with 10-foot Youngstown plug doors. Since the car was assigned to M D & W Railway and had load devices it probably is in high-class paper roll service for Boise Cascade. (Bill Phillips)

BKTY 20800; series 20656-20825; class B-70-33
73.5-ton RBL; 50'2" IL; 5040 cu. ft. WHEN EMPTY RETURN TO AGENT N & W MEXICO MO.
BKTY 20264; series 20200-20311; class B-70-33
72.5-ton RBL; 49'1" IL; 4640 cu. ft. WHEN EMPTY RETURN TO AGENT B.N. RR. KANSAS CITY, MO.

▲▼Although these cars are dimensionally the same, they have differing cubic feet, due to being equipped with different loaders. Both groups have 9-Belt Evans DF-2 utility loaders (with 20-crossmembers, 10-deckboards) and 10-foot Youngstown plug doors. At one time up to 56 cars from both series had pallets considered as part of the car for specific shippers. The lower cubic capacity for the grocery type cars 20200-20311 are because they had 2-bulkheads (Equipco or Preco brand bulkheads) and 12 or 24 panel sidewall fillers. The combination of the bulkheads and the sidewall fillers are particularly effective in securing palletized loads. Number 20800 probably was used for miscellaneous manufactured products service, like refractory products from Mexico, Missouri, while number 20264 probably was assigned for flour or other foodstuffs from Kansas City. Both groups were built by ACF between June and September 1966. The photos of cars 20800 and 20264 were taken in Fort Worth in December 1979 and in Parsons on August 14, 1977 respectively showing great underframe detail especially the HYDRA-CUSHION cylinders. *(Bill Phillips) (Richard Yaremko)*

**MKT 8984, 8977; series 8900-8999
71-ton RBL; 50'7" IL; 4668 cu. ft.**
▲ ▶ Here are examples of the red and green schemes of the same Pacific Car and Foundry built series of cars. The PC&F plant in Portland, Oregon built these cars in October 1968. Note the builder stencil below the ACI label on number 8984. These "Grocery Cars" came equipped with LD load dividers, side fillers and 10'6" exterior post Youngstown plug doors. Over half of the cars came equipped with 26, 48 or 90 pallets, probably designed to particular shipper's specifications. Number 8984 was found in Dallas in February of 1979, while number 8977 is sitting in Denison on a day in July 1982, repainted into green at the same location. *(Bill Phillips) (Steele Craver)*

**MKT 8805; series 8800-8899
86.5-ton RBL; 60'7" IL; 5583 cu. ft.**
▲This is a typical example of a later Whitman green paint scheme with stenciled yellow lettering, small reporting marks and loader symbols. These "Grocery Cars" were the largest cubic capacity the MKT purchased from PCF in November 1968. This group of cars was equipped with LD load dividers, side fillers and 10'6" exterior post Youngstown plug doors. Some cars had up to 96 pallets and a few had Dual Air-Pac load restraining devices, some of which were in dedicated beer service (Coors or Miller perhaps!). This example was found in Melrose Park, Illinois on January 19 1984.

(Raymond F. Kucaba)

MKT 20045, 20032; series 20000-20099
72-ton RBL; 50'6" IL; 5040 cu. ft.

▲▼ Pullman-Standard eventually leased RBL's to the Katy as well, when they delivered this series of 100 PS-1 design cars in March 1970. Originally delivered in the current red Barriger "Katy" scheme like the example of number 20045 in Denison, Texas on November 30th 1980. The next example of number 20032 is of a rare Whitman green "Katy" emblem in yellow in Fort Worth January 24th 1982. Like some of the previously mentioned RBL's this group of cars received a similar assortment of load restraining devices for "Grocery Cars": load dividers, bulkheads, side fillers and 10'6" Youngstown plug doors. They probably received PS Hydroframe cushioning, rather than the ever-popular HYDRA-CUSHION. *(Richard Yaremko) (Bill Phillips)*

Flat Cars and Bulkhead Flats

MKT 13517, x-1110; series 13501-13525;
55-ton FM and LP (later FMS); 53'6" IL;

◄ MKT purchased General Steel Casting frames and added the brake system, trucks and decking to them at its own shops in February 1952. They were classified initially LP and later changed to FMS. A handful of these cars had fixed cast bulkheads and a locker at one end, for plasterboard service. The locker held tape and joint compound. Our example is shown with a crane load in maintenance of way service at Hillsboro, Texas in January 1973. *(Steele Craver)*

MKT 9057; series 9050-9074; 77-ton LP (later FMS); 48'6" IL;

▲ Received from Thrall Car in January 1959 and originally numbered 50 to 74, with an AAR class of LP. These cars were renumbered and probably were re-classed to FMS sometime between late 1967 to late 1970. Like our previous example, these bulkhead flats received the then standard all black paint scheme for flat cars. The entire deck was a nailable steel floor and the "A" end (shown here on the left) had a locker to hold tie-down chains. Although by this April 1978 photo in Fort Worth, it seems that steel banding was used recently. Again MKT primarily assigned these bulkhead flats to plasterboard service. *(Steele Craver)*

MKT 14015; series 14015; 97.5-ton FMS; 46'8" IL;

◀ Built by Evans in September 1966 and captured with other coil cars in Fort Worth, Texas on September 19, 1982. These cars came equipped with special fittings to secure the coil loads of steel, covers, and end-of-car cushioning. The covers were fabricated from sheet steel. Bozo Texino strikes again! *(Bill Phillips)*

MKT 13838; series 13800-13849; 98.5-ton FM; 58'5" IL;

▶ By the time the Katy received these Evans built flat cars in December 1967 Barriger red was the paint scheme of choice. This exceptional shot shows the detail on the wooden deck and the 40-foot rails with staking, plus other details like the weathering of the wood, the end-of-car cushioning and the associated "trombone" style uncoupling lever. Number 13838 is sitting on a siding off the main in Bells, Texas. *(Steele Craver)*

MKT 13912; series 13900-13949;
95-ton FMS; 48'6" IL;
▲ One month after the previous car, MKT received another fifty cars of the same design from Evans but with the addition of bulkheads. This made the inner length 48'6", by then the industry standard for bulkhead flats. The deck and bulkhead faces were wooden and the cars came equipped with Aeroquip tie-down straps, end of car cushioning, and a locker on the "A" end of the car. Most Katy bulkhead flats were in wallboard service. Fort Worth, Texas March 21st, 1982. *(Bill Phillips)*

MKT 14003; series 14002-14003;
125-ton FM; 45'6" IL;
▼ These two cars were specially built to haul loads like the one shown to or from Westinghouse. The load is probably for the petroleum industry in Oklahoma or Texas. The builder of the 125-ton Katy car was Thrall Car back in November 1968. Note the use of four sets of standard trucks underneath the steel underframe. Bill shot this example of 14003 in Forth Worth on February 1980. *(Bill Phillips)*

MKT 13134; series 13100-13199;
98-ton FM; 60'0" IL;
▼ This car was photographed in Hampton, Texas on the 18th of July 1982, repainted in 1979 into Whitman green. It was built by Thrall and received by MKT between October and November 1968. As a bonus, this car is loaded with a Bantam RAIL ROADER crane, which is hi-rail capable.

(Bill Phillips)

**MKT 13144;
series 13121, 13144;
98-ton FMS; 60'0" IL;
WHEN EMPTY RETURN TO CONRAIL AGENT CONNELLSVILLE, PA.**

▶ These two cars come from the 13100 to 13199 series of cars built by Thrall car mentioned previously. The exception being they were specifically assigned to STEEL PLATE LOADING ONLY, therefore receiving the permanent angled carrier frame to accept wider steel plates than car.

(Craig T. Bossler)

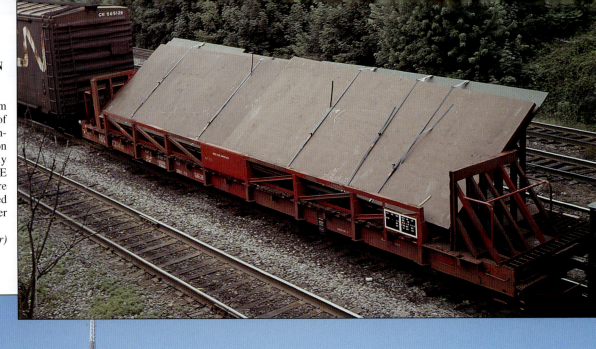

**MKT 14040; series 14025-14049;
95-ton FMS; 52'0" IL;**

▲ MKT classified these coiled cars as flat cars, whereas other railroads have classified them as special gondolas with roofs (GBSR). They were built by Ortner Freight Car Co. in February 1981 and therefore received the standard Whitman green, but the fiberglass glass covers were yellow with green stenciling. Note the yellow Scotchlite rectangles on the car sides. These cars came equipped with special fittings to secure the coil loads of steel, and end-of-car cushioning. Captured with a twin in Fort Worth, Texas on June 24 1983. *(Bill Phillips)*

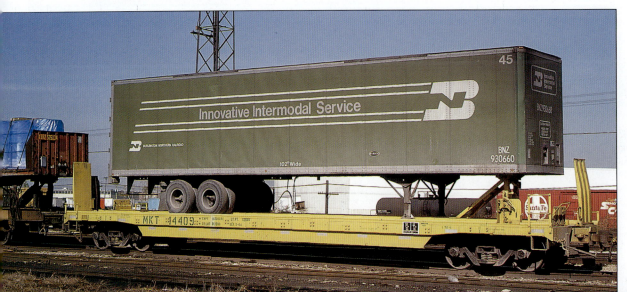

**MKT 14409;
series 14400-14599;
42.5-ton FC; 52'9" IL;**

◀ Between May 1984 and February 1985, the Denison and Parsons shops converted 200 ACF boxcars from series numbers 1900 to 2199 to these specialized piggyback flat cars. This was MKT's reaction to the increasing volume of piggyback traffic and the increased lengths of piggyback trailers.

(Ronald A. Plazzotta)

Equipped and Unequipped Gondolas

MKT 137; series 100-149; 55-ton GBS; 41'3" IL; 1749 cu. ft.

▶ These cars were named "PEEK-A-BOO" by MKT for obvious reasons, shown in Columbus, OH in May 1965. These special service gondolas were primarily used for pipe loading, but were classed to carry pulpwood as well. This car is probably headed for Pittsburgh PA for a load of pipe for the petroleum industry "back home" in Oklahoma. MKT reconditioned (making them peek-a-boo) these gons in 1959 from ex-43001 to 43500 series cars built between January and September of 1937. *(Paul C. Winters)*

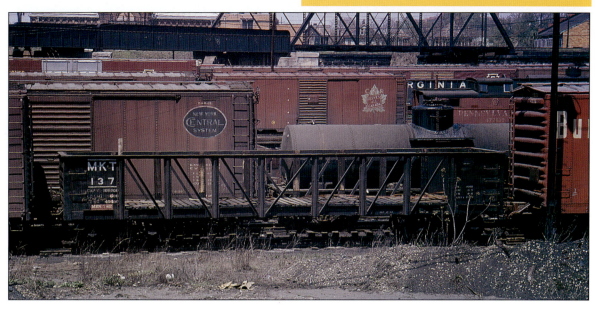

MKT 42248; series 42001-42300; 77-ton GB; 50'6" IL; 2240 cu. ft.

◀ We find number 42248 in scrap steel service in Reading, PA on August the 7th 1978. Besides the green paint applied by the Denison shops in November 1975, a top chord with gussets has been added and possibly some side sheets replaced. These 50-foot 6-inch 77-ton gondolas were built by Pullman-Standard in 1951. *(Craig T. Bossler)*

MKT 43710; series 43701-43725; 77-ton GB; 65'6" IL; 1748 cu. ft.

▲ Purchased from Bethlehem Steel in July 1966 for long steel mill products, like 20' to 60' length rebar, and hot-rolled sections like flats, squares, rounds and channels. One of MKT main customers for these cars was Armco served via the Sand Springs Railway from the Tulsa, OK area. Armco was purchased by HMK Group and renamed Sheffield Steel in 1981. This group of gons had steel floors, fixed ends and tie-downs on the top chord. Number 43710 is shown in its original paint scheme with equally sized reporting marks and numbers at opposite ends of the car. A couple of cars from the series wait on track near Sheffield Steel along US 64 in Sand Springs Oklahoma on September 25th 1982. These were the first series of 65-foot gondolas the Katy received. Another 100 cars followed from Thrall that were 2947 cubic feet and had cushioning. Ninety of the 2947 cubic feet Thrall gondolas were leased by BN Inc. and eventually left the roster by January 1975. *(Raymond F. Kucaba)*

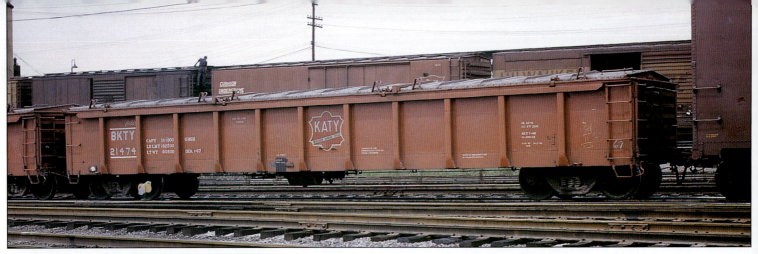

BKTY 21474, 21478; series 21450-21499; G-100-13
90.5, 82.5-ton GBSR; 52'6" IL; 2161, 2681 cu. ft.

▲▼The only gondolas that received the Barriger red with the KATY emblem were this series, which was typical for all BKTY leased cars. The three section removable roof is to cover the usual load of coiled steel. Darby Corp. built these cars in July 1966 and this example was photographed in August 1968. Unlike most coil cars this design did not have underframe or end-of-car cushioning, although they did have four moveable bulkheads inside to restrain the load. Six of them were also assigned to Glass Loading, having 4-inch wood floors. In 1978 the Denison shops extended the sides and hooking loops on the covers to some cars, as demonstrated by number 21478. This was to accommodate typically larger diameter coils, which in turn reduced the capacity but increased the cubic feet. Bill shot number 21478 in Carrollton, Texas on a day in December of 1979.

(Paul C. Winters) (Bill Phillips)

MKT 16270; series 16000-16499;
100-ton GB; 52'6" IL; 2240 cu. ft.

▼ Thrall supplied these 500 cars in the first quarter of 1970, wearing the most typical red paint scheme for gons. Bill captured number 16270 in Fort Worth on March 21st, 1982 in reasonable condition considering the abuse gondolas receive. It still has most of its original lettering, including the builder's logo. At least five cars of the group were equipped to handle ten 64 cubic foot removable drop bottom containers for Ferro-manganese ore, which is used in steel making. *(Bill Phillips)*

**MKT 16515; series 16500-16519;
100-ton GBS; 50'10" IL; 2240 cu. ft.**

▲ Another series of specially equipped gondolas were these 20 cars for pipe loading, notice the high fixed ends with a pipe load. The pipes were probably headed toward Katy country for the petroleum industry in Texas and Oklahoma. The Katy's Denison shops have repainted this car in October 1979, over nine years after they were built in March 1970. We find number 16515 in McCook, Illinois on the 16th of December 1981.

(Raymond F. Kucaba)

**MKT 12447; series 12400-12499 (2nd);
100-ton GB; 52'6" IL; 2245 cu. ft.**

▲ The first use of these numbers was for 52-foot six-inch gondolas built by Thrall in 1967. Their specifications were 97.5 tons 2240 cubic foot capacity, and had steel floors, fixed ends and end-of-car cushioning. They were leased by BN Inc. in the early seventies and treated as BN cars with all per diem charges and all other reporting directed toward BN Inc. One month old 12447 is shot in Fort Worth with what looks like others from the same series of gons. The Whitman green and yellow M K T initials are quite striking when new and the data is legible enough to make out a built date of August 1979, as is the blue and white Ortner Freight Car Co. builder's plate. These 100 cars were placed into general service duties and featured steel floors, fixed ends and angle iron welded on the top chord, a typical MKT application. *(Bill Phillips)*

Open Hoppers

**MKT 905; series 900-911;
70-ton HT; 40'8" IL;
2622 cu. ft.**

◀ In the early 1960's MKT purchased 12 cars from the Chesapeake & Ohio. The C&O series (5,250 in total) were built new in 1956 by the C&O Raceland Car Shops. This example was built in December and has remnants of the yellow Futura Demi-bold scheme with MKT reporting marks and number. Our photographer found number 905 in the dead lines of Ray Yard in Denison sometime in January 1971. *(Steele Craver)*

MKT 10554; series 10000-10599; 100-ton HT; 45'0" IL; 3600 cu. ft.

◄ MKT purchased many hoppers for coal service, like these 600 hoppers built between February and June 1967. This series of hoppers plus two additional series; 10600-10899 and 15000-15399 were leased to the UP in early 1969 for a start-up of the Kaiser Steel unit train between Sunnyside, UT (DRGW) and Fontana, CA (ATSF). The cars were returned to MKT when UP and DRGW Thrall gondolas were delivered in mid-1969. The 3600 cubic foot hoppers would be useful for the less dense western coal probably from Wyoming via the Burlington Northern, Colorado & Southern and Forth Worth and Denver railroads. By the time of this November 2nd 1980 photo, number 10554 has received modifications to the top chord gussets at the end of the ribs. *(Bill Phillips)*

MKT 15334; series 15000-15499; 100-ton HT; 45'0" IL; 3600 cu. ft.

▼ Another large group of cars (at least for the Katy) of 500 hoppers were built by Bethlehem Steel Co. during June and July 1968. Carrying a load of black diamonds, our example is found in Colorado Springs, CO during December of 1969. Katy hoppers built during this time wore the red with white 30" M K T, number 15334 being an excellent example. Note the angle iron welded to the top of the chord for added strength. Some time between May 1970 and January 1972 Burlington Northern Inc. leased this series of cars (15000-15499 to BN 523000-523399) and another (10600-10899 to BN 522400-522699). These cars were treated as if they had BN markings and all per diem and reporting should be directed to BN Inc. Some of MKT's hoppers were also used for stone, gravel and ores, with significant on-line business of each. *(Jim Eager collection)*

MKT 10950; series 10900-10999; 100-ton HT; 49'3" IL; 3430 cu. ft.

◄ MKT had many on-line utilities, especially in the state of Texas, and ran quite a few unit trains. Therefore, the railroad needed large order numbers compared to other car types. These 100 cars were a follow-on order from Trinity in 1979 from an almost identical 100 cars in series, 10800 to 10899. The coal is rolling in Parsons, KS on September 3, 1981, the hoppers were delivered in Whitman green with a nearly full-height yellow M K T. *(Ronald A. Plazzotta)*

Covered Hoppers Two-Bay Covered Hoppers

**MKT 34022;
series 34001-34100
77-ton LO; 29'9" IL;
1958 cu. ft.**

◀ We start with the latest paint scheme on these 1950-built cars from Pressed Steel Car. There is no guessing what lading these cars carried; we catch up with 34022 in Saint Louis, Missouri on June the 2nd, 1977, probably delivering the glass sand for beer bottles for a well-known beverage maker in town. The Katy served a large silica sand region in Oklahoma where this car will probably be going after it is empty. Note the good condition of the eight square hatches on top as well as the car body in general.
(Raymond F. Kucaba)

**MKT 34264; series 34201-34275
MKT 34375; series 34301-34375
77-ton LO; 29'9" IL; 2003 cu. ft.**

▲▶ The next two groups of covered hoppers were built by Pullman-Standard at their Milton, PA plant. The first group were delivered in August 1955, whilst the second in January 1956. Another example of Katy's care of its equipment, we find number 34264 in Denison in late 1980 with its original grey paint scheme. Number 34375 is also in Denison, but nearly six years later in May 1986 in re-paint red. Besides the slight upgrading of cubic capacity, they came with 30" circular hatches that are ideal for sealing moisture from the typical load of cement. Note a little cement built up around the hatches for both. The MKT advertised these cars to also carry commodities like fertilizer, fly ash, silica sand or feed. It seems that graffiti artist Bozo Texino really enjoyed MKT equipment for his signatures; you will see his work throughout this book. Bozo Texino is a nickname made up by a Missouri Pacific engineer. *(both, Richard Yaremko)*

**BKTY 1311, 1300;
series 1300-1374; class H-100-17
100-ton LO; 29'3" IL; 2600 cu. ft.**
▲▶ These 100-ton cars are leased covered covered hoppers from Bankers Leasing Corporation; the Pullman-Standard Butler, PA plant built them in February 1966. Numbers 1300 to 1320 were assigned for calcium carbide loading, while the numbers 1321 to 1374 were specifically for cement. Both of our examples are the calcium carbide assigned cars and display the original red and later green paint. Notice the stenciling on 1300 referencing the lading and its FLAMMABLE SOLID placard. There is a large calcium carbide manufacturer on-line in Pryor, OK, Midwest Carbide Corp., ideally located to sources of petroleum coke and hydro-electricity from the Grand River Dam Authority (GRDA).
(both, Bill Phillips)

**MKT 403;
series 400-499;
100-ton LO;
34'9" IL; 2980 cu. ft.**
◀ This 100-ton "Center Flow" covered hopper was ordered by ACF in November 1979. The car is so new the galvanized Morton roof walks are still shiny and the trucks show their black paint. These cars had four loading hatches and two gravity outlets. Our example is found in brilliant green and yellow only two months after it was built, resting in the Dallas yard.
(Bill Phillips)

Three-Bay Covered Hoppers

MKT 293; series 285-294
77-ton LO; 41'3" IL; 3510 cu. ft.

▲ Before red being introduced to covered hoppers the prevalent color was grey as shown in our example in Denison, Texas on May 25th, 1985. These ten cars were built in July of 1964 by the American Car and Foundry Huntington plant. Before the large cubic capacity cars, this type of car could be used in grain or fertilizer service, but was probably demoted to fertilizer-only by this date. *(Richard Yaremko)*

BKTY 1012; series 1000-1029; class H-70-24
78-ton LO; 41'2" IL; 3500 cu. ft.
WHEN EMPTY RETURN TO MKT AGENT PRYOR OKLA.

▼ These 78-ton cars are the first leased covered hoppers from Bankers Leasing Corporation; the ACF Huntington plant built them in December 1965. This series has six circular hatches and three gravity outlets, useful for grain or fertilizer. This car has probably been recently carrying fertilizer note the tape remaining from warning labels and white spill from the hatches. As with most BKTY cars, these covered hoppers received the typical red Barriger paint scheme including the "KATY" emblem. The Katy served Wil-Gro Fertilizer Inc. (Originally John Deere Chemical Co. the tractor manufacturer) in Pryor, Oklahoma. *(Bill Phillips)*

BKTY 1152;
series 1150-1154;
class H-100-16
99.5-ton LO; 49'6" IL;
4427 cu. ft.

◀ Pullman-Standard built this small group of their popular PS-2 4427 cf. covered hoppers in February 1966 for lease to MKT. Number 1152 was captured in Kansas City in August 12th 1984. As with most Barriger paint scheme cars, the red in the logo decal weathered very well compared to the paint turning a brown. This series has six hatches and three gravity-pneumatic outlets. Being such a small series of covered hoppers and equipped with specific outlets they probably were purchased with a specific load and shipper in mind. *(Peter Arnold)*

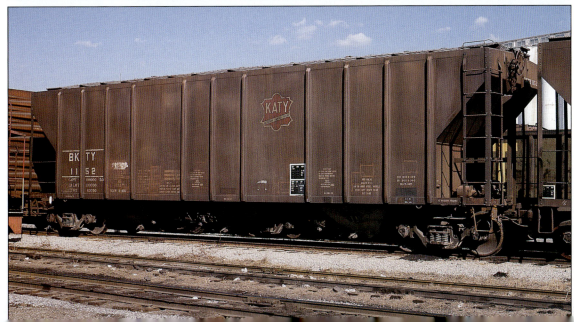

**MKT 9348; series 9200-9599;
100-ton LO; 49'9" IL; 4450 cu. ft.**

▲ MKT needed 100-ton covered hoppers for the grain rush toward the Gulf; these 400 cars from Thrall Car arrived between June and August 1967. The Barriger paint scheme had been simplified to the 30" high white "M K T" which started a trend for all covered hoppers. Not since a four-car 1964 PS order of 4427 cubic foot covered hoppers (MKT 320-323, assigned specifically for malt) had Katy covered hoppers received trough hatches and three gravity outlets. Note that additional ribs were welded on the body and around the hoppers compared to the PS equivalents. *(Bill Phillips)*

**MKT 9611; series 9600-9899;
100-ton LO; 49'6" IL; 4427 cu. ft.**

▼ MKT needed additional 100-ton covered hoppers so this time they went to Pullman-Standard for 300 cars, receiving them April to May 1968. Richard Yaremko captured number 9611 in good condition in Fort Worth on the 16th of March 1980. Like the previous Thrall cars, these received trough hatches and three gravity outlets with the simplified paint scheme and 30" high white "M K T". The MKT Freight Equipment shippers guide listed the typical ladings as grain and fertilizer. *(Richard Yaremko)*

**MKT 4002; series 4000-4099;
100-ton LO; 48'9" IL; 4650 cu. ft.**

▲ MKT went to another lease company, BT Leasing Services Inc. (Owner and Lessor) for these 100 cars in late 1975 or January 1976. They originally had CKIX reporting marks and were built at the ACF Huntington plant in May 1975. Note the original marks and numbers have been over-painted with the new ones for MKT. Steele captured number 4002 very soon after delivery to the Katy in Fort Worth, Texas in January 1976. These Plate C cars were equipped with four-piece FRP continuous hatches and three bolted-on gravity outlets. *(Steele Craver)*

**MKT 4192; series 4100-4199;
100-ton LO; 54'1" IL; 4780 cu. ft.**

▼ These Evans 100-ton, Plate C covered hoppers arrived in green with large yellow "M K T" in February 1978. Note the loading levels markings, which indicate the levels for different commodities to help the loaders not to overload beyond 100-tons, they have trough hatches and three gravity outlets. Fort Worth Texas April 26th 1981. *(Bill Phillips)*

**MKT 4428;
series 4300-4599;
100-ton LO;
53'3" IL; 4750 cu. ft.**

▶ This perfectly lit shot of number 4428 highlights all the frame details and brake rigging of these 100-ton PS design Trinity-built cars. It was photographed in the low April sun in 1983 in San Luis Obispo, California. The 300 cars, built in October 1980, all had trough hatches, three gravity outlets and the standard green scheme including reflector rectangles on the bottom angle.
(Peter Arnold)

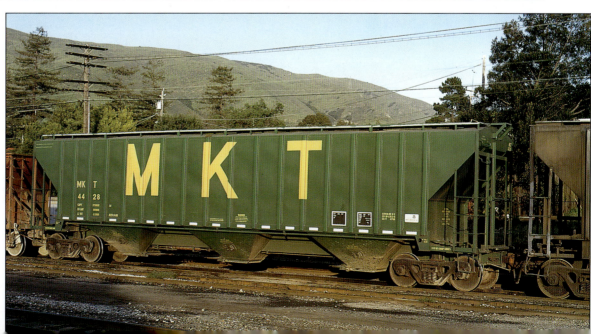

Airslide Covered Hoppers

MKT 9035; series 9016-9035;
BKTY 1053; series 1050-1053; class H-70-24; 77-ton LO; 29'6" IL; 2600 cu.

▲▼ General American developed and built the Airslide covered hopper to carry dense materials like sugar, flour, starch, feldspar and cement. The Katy used theirs for sugar and flour loads. The first example was built in January 1959 the second in March 1966; both had six hatches and two outlets. Other design details had changed over the seven years, notably the replacement of the end channels with ribs and the addition of gussets between the end sheets and the side plate. The Katy eventually received twenty-five 2600 cubic foot cars in total, numbered in three groups, the third being MKT 295-299 built in 1964. Number 9035 was captured at Ray Yard in Denison May 1975, while number 1053 was found in Hodge, Texas on August 15 1982. *(Steele Craver) (Bill Phillips)*

MKT 9108;
series 9100-9130;
94.5-ton LO;
48'11" IL; 4180 cu. ft.

▶ MKT also ordered two groups of the ten-hatch four-outlet 4180 cubic foot Airslide as well, for a total of 69 cars. The other series not shown here were leased; BKTY 1200-1228 built in October 1966 and received originally in the Barriger red scheme. This rare downward shot in Enola, PA on May 17th, 1986 clearly shows the unusual layout of the ten hatches and ribs on the roof. *(Craig T. Bossler)*

Autoracks

RTTX 474929; flat class F85b
FC; 85'0" IL;
WHEN EMPTY RETURN TO NYC RR FAIRLANE, OHIO
▲ Hubcap-less Ford Falcons fill the three fixed levels of THE TRANSPORTER KATY rack, built by The Darby Corporation. The F-85-B flat car was built by Pullman-Standard during December 1960. Note the extra long bridge plates, the end of car cushioning and the "F" (probably denoting Ford service) on a gusset below the Deramus Katy logo. This beautiful shot was captured east of Ewing Street in St. Louis Missouri in 1963. *(Paul C. Winters)*

TTRX 962887; flat class Bsh11
64-ton FA; 89'4" IL;
▼ Welded onto this longer, Bethlehem built flush-deck flatcar was another Darby built rack, but the construction was much lighter than our previous example. It seems as if the original rack design needed improving as can be seen with the cross brace additions. This car is loaded with the German built Ford Fiesta's on the first two levels and Ford light trucks on top. Richard Yaremko caught this auto rack in Ferris, Texas, and March 15 1980. *(Richard Yaremko)*

**TTKX 802733;
flat class Plh10
40-ton FA; 89'4" IL;**

▶ Auto racks were successful in regaining a majority of auto traffic but one of the drawbacks was that they were vulnerable to vandalism. The reaction by the railroads was to add protective side panels, like this example found empty at Denison in August 1984. This low-deck flat was built by Pullman-Standard (class Plh-10) in March 1974 and the Whitehead & Kales rack has a hinged middle deck to provide clearance when loading. *(Richard Yaremko)*

**TTBX 942194;
flat class Psh21
61-ton FA; 89'4" IL;**

◀ The next step for protection by the railroad industry was fully protected sides like this W & K-built bi-level rack. This P-S flush-deck flat was built in November 1977 in TTX yellow, while the rack is painted green minus the galvanized pressed steel panels. This rack is loaded with Ford trucks and probably is coming from a plant in Kansas City. Photographed in Hodge TX August 1982. The MKT did not serve the Ford plant directly (or any others) but The Katy forwarded a large amount of auto traffic from Ford and GM. *(Bill Phillips)*

**TTGX 254779;
flat class Psh20
57.5-ton FA;
89'4" IL;**

▶ This all yellow fully enclosed bi-level rack built by Whitehead & Kales in April 1985 is captured in Kansas City MO on May 14 1989. It is probably carrying trucks like the auto rack next to it. The green MKT with yellow background is applied to a perforated galvanized panel, unlike the previous example on a solid sheet. *(Roger Bee)*

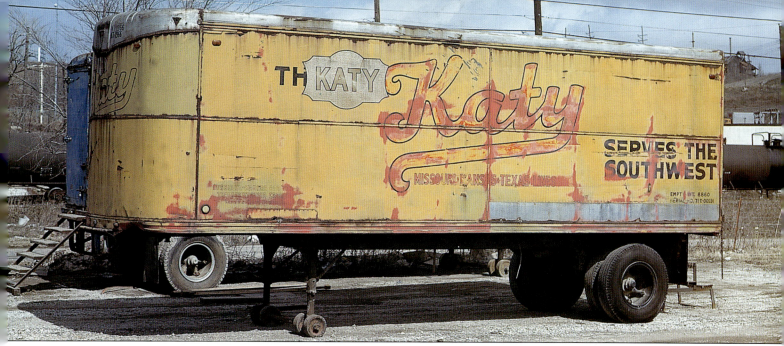

Trailers

KT-1966; Z; 24'0" OL;
▲ This 24-foot Trailmobile trailer is a survivor in Kansas City, with two paint schemes and in good body condition. It is probably in maintenance of way service by this March 1984 date. These trailers were originally purchased for LCL starting in 1954 and extended to piggyback service later. Trailmobile built them during the early fifties. *(Ronald A. Plazzotta)*

MKTZ 704072; series 704070-704073 Z; 40'0" OL; Insulated; 2418 cu. ft.
▼ The Katy developed a separate logo for its piggyback service with a family reminder using the MKT emblem outline. These insulated trailers were built by Brown and were 12-foot 6-inch high. This very well lit shot highlights all the details mounted on a flat in Parsons, Kansas on August 13, 1977.
(Richard Yaremko)

MKTZ 205086; series 205061-205089 Z; 40'0" OL; 2680 cu. ft.
▶ MKTZ 205086 is rolling by in Fort Worth, Texas on 19 September 1981. Dorsey built this group of 40-foot by 13-foot 6-inch high trailers.
(Richard Yaremko)

Tractors

KATY TRANSPORT CO. G-181;
▶ A red International Harvester model R-185 numbered G-181 found resting in Muskogee, Oklahoma in July 1978. The pale yellow Katy cowhide logo had MK&T TRANS. CO. in between the double lines.
(Richard Yaremko)

COORDINATED TRANSPORTION CO.;
◀ Coordinated Transportation Company was a wholly owned subsidiary company created to handle all terminal and delivery services for MKT piggyback service. This Diamond Reo is in view of rails in Denison, Texas November 1980. Note that the emblem is in a reflective gold and has the words Katy and COORDINATED below.
(Richard Yaremko)

COORDINATED TRANSPORTION CO.;
▶ This Ford LNT-9000 has a yellow emblem with Katy and KATY TRANS. CO. in between the ribbon below. It seems this Ford is attending to a wreck clean up at Roanoke, Texas rather than its typical duties on this sunny day on May 25th, 1985. *(Richard Yaremko)*

Non-Revenue Equipment

Cranes, Derricks and Pile Drivers

MKT X-1220, X-101337;
60-ton; Wrecking Crane and Water & Tender car
▶ This rare color slide from July 19, 1948 taken near the turntable pit in Houston TX, shows a classic steam wrecking crane. This 60-ton wrecker with a 25-foot boom was created in 1905 by Industrial. Note the Tender car following is fully laden with coal and probably water in the tank below ready for its next assignment. *(R. Fillman)*

MKT X-256, X-2317, X-76999;
125-ton;
Wrecking Crane and Boom cars
◀ This 125-ton Industrial-Brownhoist 1958-built diesel crane rests on the Parsons wrecker track with Boom cars in May 1970. The right side Boom car seems to have originated as an outside-braced boxcar while the other probably started life as a gondola. *(Owen Leander)*

KATY
▶ This Hendrickson truck with crane deserves to be with the railroad cranes. The truck attends to LNER's *Flying Scotsman* on its historic two-year visit to North America. The *Scotsman* tour ran on MKT rails between Temple, TX and Kansas City, needing repairs in Waco, Texas in June 1970. *(Emery J. Gulash)*

MKT 100288; MWM; Crew car
◀ Converted from a 40-foot PS-1 boxcar for the crane/pile driver crew, providing them with shelter from the cold or the hot southwest sun. Note the smoke jack on the far left corner for the stove. The crew car is between jobs in Texas on an overcast day in November 1979. *(Tony Lovasz)*

MKT 1031, 100203; MWF; Crane/Pile Driver, Boom car;
▶ American Hoist & Derrick crane and pile driver with its boom car resting on the same day. It was built in 1957 and still in it's original paint. The boom car is an ex-flatcar, numbers 13501 to 13525, built by MKT in 1952 with a GSC cast underframe.
(Tony Lovasz)

MKT 1031; Crane/Pile Driver
◀ The same crane is working with a bucket in Dallas on November 22nd 1984. The vehicle is a self-propelled diesel-electric crane and pile driver and very versatile in doing maintenance jobs along the right of way.
(Bill Phillips)

Work Gang Cars

**MKT X-2121;
43'0" IL; Bunk Car**

◀ This original 34-foot boxcar was built around 1917. The car was rebuilt by the MKT shops in November 1944, painted in this attractive Sloan yellow paint scheme and photographed in 1945 by noted color pioneer Emery J. Gulash. The bunk car contained fourteen bunks and rode on Arch Bar trucks. Note the water tank on the roof; it looks like an ex-air cylinder. *(Emery J. Gulash)*

**MKT 100200;
MWP; 71'10" IL;
Work Car**

▶ Originally built by ACF in 1937 or 1938 as a Chair Car from the 901 to 925 series. We find it in freshly painted Katy red on May 15 1970 in Parsons, Kansas. It probably was used as a mobile kitchen and diner for the track gangs on the road, note the window-hung air-conditioner necessary for the southwest summers.

(Owen Leander)

**MKT 100286;
MWM; 50'7" IL;
Troop Sleeper/
Bunk Car**

◀ Following WWII, many railroads had purchased Troop Sleeper cars like our example. This one was built by Pullman-Standard sometime between 1943 and 1945. The resourceful Miss Katy retained a few of these cars as bunk cars for road gangs; after all they did have 18 bunks already installed. Number 100286 was ex-number x-2402 and rides on Allied Full Cushioned trucks.

(Bill Phillips)

Ballast Cars

**MKT 40600, 40526; series 40501-40600;
70-ton HK; 40'5" IL; 2446 cu. ft.**
▲ A string of these General American Car Co. ballast hoppers built in 1930 and re-weighed at Ray yard in July 1944 photographed at an unknown location in the 1950's. They were built at the General American East Chicago, Illinois plant and were at one time numbered in the x10001 to x10099 series. Unusual for hoppers, the Katy used the "The Katy SERVING THE SOUTHWEST" slogan and brown paint. *(Emery J. Gulash)*

**MKT 100000; series 100000-100099;
97.5-ton HK; 43'0" IL; 2650 cu. ft.**
▼ Part of President Barriger's Katy recovery plan of 1965 was to improve the right of way. These 100 ballast cars were built in December 1966 wearing this red paint scheme were a step toward that goal. This group of cars was built by FMC-Gunderson from Portland, Oregon, the first time MKT ordered from them.
(Bill Phillips)

Miscellaneous Equipment

**MKT 77191;
MWM; 40'6" IL;
3128 cu. ft.; Tool Car**

◀ We find this tool car laying over in Ray Yard Denison, Texas in reasonable condition considering it was built by ACF in 1923. Reconditioned in 1964 in the company shops by adding end doors, a doorstep under the National bottom hung six-foot door, and some metal sheeting on the lower wooden planks. The Katy selected a few cars from the 76001-77500 series for this type of service.

(Steele Craver)

**MKT 34064; MWM;
29'3" IL; 1958 cu. ft.;
Sand Car COMPANY
SAND ONLY LOAD
& RETURN TO
GENERAL STORE
KEEPER PARSONS
KANSAS**

▶ Another car painted in maintenance of way brown is sitting on the Parsons (Kansas) sand track in May 1976. Its vintage is from a group of 100 covered hoppers built by Pressed Steel Car Co. in September 1950, series 34001 to 34100. From the stenciling there is no mistake to this cars assignment and it's contents of company sand.

(Steele Craver)

**MKT 100101;
50-ton MWF;
53'6" IL; Wheel Car**

◀ This flat car came from a group of American Car and Foundry April 1954 built flat cars, series 13701 to 13725. It seems to have been converted by the Denison shops in March 1960 and assigned to wheel service. It's doing just that as it rolls into or out of Parsons on September the 3rd, 1981. Parsons was one of the major shops on the system.

(Ronald A. Plazzotta)

MKT 100189;
10,000 gal. 50-ton MWT; 32'5" IL; Used Lube Oil Car
▲ With a less than glamorous Dallas skyline in the background on May 12 1974, Bill captured number 100189 enjoying the sun. The tank car built by ACF in September 1920 and assigned for waste lube oil. It must have been repainted since 1920 considering its condition and the application of the Barriger red KATY scheme. *(Bill Phillips)*

MKT 310; series 300-319;
19,000 gal. 77-ton MWT; 51'11" IL; Used Lube Oil Car
▼ WHEN EMPTY RETURN TO GENERAL STORE KEEPER PARSONS KANS. Our next example is a modern version of the same car, also built by American Car and Foundry, but in March 1959. The tank cars in this series have received three paint schemes since they were built. The subject details are highlighted while outside the main shop building well lit by an afternoon sun in March 1984. *(Raymond F. Kucaba)*

MKT 1045;
INSPECTION CAR
▶ This weird but "cute" car was an ingenious invention by VP of Operations Bishop, constructed from a boxcar at the Denison shops in 1973. It was used as an Inspection Car to tour the MKT system, although it rode like a boxcar it had all the modern conveniences such as air-conditioning and comfortable chairs. Of course Bill Phillips was at hand to snap this shot of Number 1045 at Denison, Texas a day after Christmas in 1973. *(Bill Phillips)*

Cabooses

MKT 69; series 60-69; NE; 28'1" IL;
◀ The first caboose is also the oldest caboose built in June 1928, but it happens to be in the latest Whitman green paint scheme. They received radio equipment during the repainting. They were rebuilt over a very long period by Denison between June 1959 to January 1961 only utilizing the steel underframe of the original caboose picked from the 751 to 795 series of cupola cabooses. The original group of thirty cabooses came from the same Denison company shops. The quality of the Denison shop forces workmanship with this surviving example until this April 10th 1983 Dallas, Texas photo.
(Bill Phillips, Roger Bee collection)

MKT 45; series 31-53; NE; 28'3" IL;
▶ In a state of disuse on a siding in Dublin, Texas on April 29th 1975 and not going anywhere but to the dead line, this classic Katy outside-braced caboose was constructed by MKT in 1930 with wood sheathing, original number series 796 to 820. They were reconditioned from 1957 to 1959 by replacing the wood sheathing with plywood sheets and painting it in the Barriger red scheme. At one time number 45 was radio equipped even though it doesn't advertise the fact.
(Bill Phillips, Roger Bee collection)

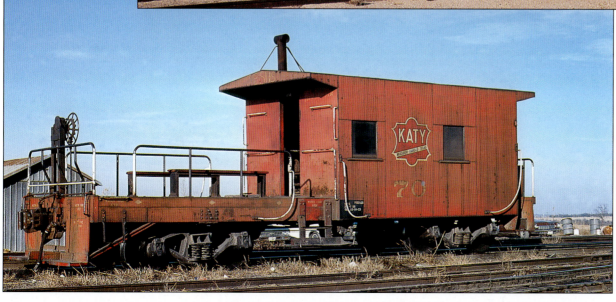

MKT 70; series 70-71; NE;
◀ Numbers 70 and 71 were utilized as yard cabooses at Ray Yard in Denison, where Bill Phillips found one of them on November 30, 1975. It is unknown what cars were sacrificed to construct these cabooses but they were from 1930 built cars. The Katy shops rebuilt a couple of unknown 1930 built cars during 1966 and 1967.
(Bill Phillips, Roger Bee collection)

**MKT 861;
series 841-870;
NE; 30'7" IL;**

◀ These cabooses were built by Denison shops from boxcars in series 74105 to 75597. They retained their steel underframes and Hutchins roof, but received Andrews type trucks. It sits at an unknown location in August 1968 wearing a very plain Sloan yellow paint scheme.

(Ronald A. Plazzotta)

MKT 73; series 73-75; NE; 17'4" IL;

▲ As a need for transfer cabooses in the Kansas City area arose, MKT went back to its shop forces to create these three cabooses. This car is believed to have been built from a boxcar numbered 41100 and 2613 from October 1945 as marked on the underframe. Number 73 was resting between transfer jobs in Kansas City, Kansas on August 25th, 1985. Note the homebuilt bench seating on the long porches. As of July 2001, this caboose was being used by the Mississippi shortline Kosciusko & Southwestern Railway. *(Bill Phillips)*

**MKT 204;
series 201-211;
NE; 29'9" IL;**

◀ This series of cabooses has a long history as well. The origins date back to 1949 when MKT built them into the 1001 to 1025 series, perhaps from another type of car. They later received upgrading and were renumbered into the 6 to 30 series. Then they had a major rebuild in 1979 at the Denison facilities, where a homebuilt wide-vision cupola replaced the standard width cupola. The end steps and platforms were replaced with a version mimicking the contemporary International Car Co. cabooses and an angle was welded to the sill stringing the bolsters and cross-braces.

(Bill Phillips)

MKT 1006; series 1001-1025; NE; 29'9" IL;
▲ This is "CLASSIC" KATY Sloan yellow with the classic slogan of "The Katy SERVES THE SOUTHWEST". What makes it more classic is the scene captured by Emery Gulash at the main diamond and tower in Tulsa, Oklahoma where we find 1006 just crossing over the Frisco main tracks in June 1964. Note the use of kerosene marker lights, the trainman in the cupola, and the extent of 1964 graffiti. Built in 1949 by MKT, it is not clear if they started from another type of car. Numbers 1001 to 1014 received radio equipment when built. *(Emery J. Gulash)*

MKT 10; series 6-30; NE; 29'9" IL;
▼ Caboose number 10 is an example of the upgrades and renumbering that were mentioned previously. They were renumbered from the 1001 to 1025 series cabooses, which occurred sometime during the Barriger period. The upgrades included blanking windows and screening the remaining ones and adding roller bearings to the wheels. Lensed on January 26th 1975 in Dallas, Texas.
(Bill Phillips)

MKT 212; series 212-215; NE; 29'9" IL;

◀This is another example of cabooses with their origins dating back to 1949 when MKT built them into the 1001 to 1025 series, then renumbered into the 6 to 30 series. Numbers 212 to 215 had a major rebuild in 1979 at the Denison facilities, where a homebuilt wide-vision cupola replaced the standard-width cupola in the same position. Green 212 waits for its next assignment in Fort Worth, August 16 1981. *(Bill Phillips, Roger Bee collection)*

MKT 4; series 1-4; NE; 28'7" IL;

▶These were the first purchased cabooses, ordered from Thrall Car Co. in June 1959. They were considered transfer cabooses, having no cupola or bay window and more importantly not radio equipped. The red (fading to pink!) Deramus era paint scheme is still hanging-on in this September 1st, 1978 Kansas City photo. Most of this group of cabooses eventually received the Barriger red as well as the Whitman green schemes.
(Bill Phillips)

MKT 5; series 5; NE;

◀This one of a kind transfer caboose built at the MKT shops in May 1961. It is unknown the origins of this car, perhaps starting out as a 40-foot car. Katy needed more transfer cabooses to service heavy transfer runs in Kansas City, the Dallas/Ft. Worth metroplex, and St. Louis areas; the latter is where we find number 5 on April 15th 1975. Eventually purchased by the Midland Railway Historical Association in Baldwin Kansas, it still exists as their number 55 in excursion service.
(Roger Bee collection)

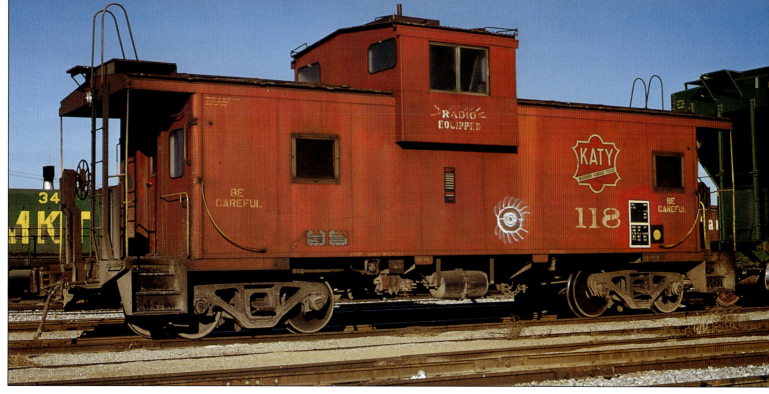

MKT 118; series 100-124; NE; 30'1" IL;
▲ Part of President Barriger's master plan to resurrect the Katy was better train service in this case with twenty-five state-of-art cabooses from International Car Company. Some of the state-of-art features include end-of-car cushioning, radio equipped (adequately advertised), and roller bearing leaf spring trucks. The frame and body including the wide-vision cupola consisted of all welded construction, allowing increased strength for longer and heavier trains, especially coal trains. The radio equipment has a Motorola "firecracker" style antenna on an isolating platform on the cupola rooftop; note the vents for the radio batteries below the left side window. MKT has recently applied the single red marker light in this October 1978 photo taken in Fort Worth. It is a pity that the "weird eye" graffiti has ruined this otherwise excellent example of the original red paint scheme. *(Bill Phillips)*

MKT 107; series 100-124; NE; 30'1" IL;
▼ Repainted in this beautiful example of Whitman green and yellow, we find number 107 hanging on the end of a train in Dallas on this September 27 1975 day. MKT received these International Car Co. cabooses between January and May 1966. The Katy added to the safety yellow end chevrons with red automotive reflectors on the roof end panels and side sills, and with red square paddles in place of marker lights. This side of the caboose clearly shows the smoke jack position, toolbox slung between the trucks and the diesel fuel-filler pipe below the cupola. ICC used a riveted overhanging diagonal panel Standard Railway Co. (Stanray) roof; note the overhang on the eves. *(Peter Arnold collection)*

MKT 132; series 125-134; NE; 30'5" IL;
▲ MKT stayed close to home for the next ten cabooses, by having The Darby Corporation of Kansas City, Kansas build them from December 1968 to June 1969. This view highlights some of the features of these wide-vision cabs: end-of-car cushioning, high mounted toilet window with vent above, large battery vents, smooth welded roof, and radio equipped (Motorola "firecracker"). Bill Phillips snapped a rich red number 132 idle in the Dallas yard on March the 11th, 1978.

MKT 76; series 125-134; NE; 30'5" IL;
▼ MKT embraced the spirit of the United States of America Bicentennial celebrations with its repainting of this caboose and a matching GP40 appropriately numbered #200. Probably still smelling of fresh paint, found on this sunny September 29th day in 1975 in Dallas. Number 76 was previously numbered 130, randomly selected from the original series. *(Bill Phillips)*

MKT 140; series 135-142; NE; 30'1" IL;
◀ In 1973, MKT placed another order with International Car Co. for an additional eight wide-vision type cabooses. Constructed by the ICC Kenton, Ohio plant, they received welded overhanging X-panel Stanray roofs and low clearance wide-vision cupolas. All of MKT's cabooses received three steps up to the end platforms, including this example. Note the two ash collectors under the side sill, inline below the smoke jack and stove. This series of cabooses were delivered in the green scheme with small "MKT".
(Ronald A. Plazzotta)

SLSF 1234, 1723;
▲ Roger Bee has captured this beautiful and timeless photo, in April 1978 near Springfield at the heart of the Frisco system. Springfield is known as the Queen City of the Ozarks and is the crossroads where the four mainlines converge: from St. Louis, Memphis, Tulsa and Kansas City. Here we see cabooses 1234 and 1723 demonstrate the typical Frisco mainline pool cabooses of the late seventies. Number 1234 is a pioneer for "wide-vision" cabooses in caboose red, the other in mandarin red and white and homebuilt. *Frisco Fast Freight! Ship it on the Frisco! (Roger Bee)*

FRISCO Equipped and Unequipped Boxcars

40-Foot Boxcars

SLSF 150418; series 150000-150999
50-ton XM; 40'6" IL; 3660 cu. ft.; "AA"
LOADING ONLY SEE
INTERIOR STENCIL

▶ We start off the Frisco section with this excellent shot by Bernie Wooller in Huntsville, Alabama on a clear November day in 1964. Pullman and Mt. Vernon Car Co. built this series of 1000 general service boxcars in 1926. This car has been refurbished in 1958, which included replacement of the wood side lining with steel, new interior wood sheathing and door with plywood. They retained their Miner Ideal lever hand brakes, steel Murphy ends and Hutchins roof, and wood running boards. Number 150418 shows a clean and classic fifties Frisco paint job with a 48" black background Coonskin and over- and underlined reporting marks and number.

(Bernie Wooller)

SLSF 162034, 162386;
series 161500-162499
55-ton XM; 40'6" IL; 2933 cu. ft.

◀ It is the summer of 1968 in Frisco's Yale yard (Memphis, Tennessee) and we find two Howe Truss boxcars from a group of 1000 cars. They are post-1933 reconditioned examples of the original Pullman Co. order from April and May 1930. The wood sheathing was replaced with steel; otherwise they originally were constructed with six-foot Youngstown sliding doors and Stanray Dreadnaught ends. Some of these cars received Murphy Improved steel roofs. Frisco was probably the first to apply the Murphy Improved roofs anywhere in May 1932, even before any manufacturer had applied them in 1933 (Pressed Steel Car Co.).

(Howard L. Robins)

SLSF 162736; series 162500-163999
50-ton XM; 40'6" IL; 2933 cu. ft.;
"AA" LOADING ONLY
SEE INTERIOR STENCIL

▶ The Frisco received an identical order from American Car & Foundry in April and May of 1930 with the following series of cars. Amazingly, Roger Taylor has captured this re-sheathed Howe Truss boxcar on April the 6th of 1998 in Enid, Oklahoma, 68 years later! This car's paint has stood the test of time, which is indicative of Frisco's care of its equipment. This is another example of the Frisco shop forces handy work with the steel sheathing installed in June of 1959. The six-foot plywood refurbished door is original to an earlier series of car, since ACF delivered this group with Youngstown corrugated doors. *(Roger Taylor)*

SLSF 32231; series 32000-32499
50-ton XM; 40'6" IL; 2933 cu. ft.
FOR "AA" LOADING ONLY SEE INTERIOR STENCIL
▲ Between 1953 and 1960 the Frisco rebuilt and renumbered a number of 1930 PS or ACF built Howe Truss boxcars in the 161500 to 163999 series. Part of the rebuilding process was replacing the sheathing with steel and relining of the interior for food grade lading. The Springfield shops applied them with a new "billboard" paint scheme, which may have been a light yellow color. It's believed to be the first use of the "SOUTHEAST-SOUTHWEST…SHIP IT ~ FRISCO" slogan on any group of equipment. The coonskin size varied from 48" applied above the reporting marks or like this 72" coonskin example on sheet steel between frame posts. There were at least ten cars in the group that received roof hatches. Number 32231 was nearly underneath the Ewing St. footbridge in the TRRA 23rd St. yard, Saint Louis, MO. This overhead view gives us an excellent vantage point of the Hutchins roof, six-foot Youngstown door, and Ajax power hand brake. *(Paul C. Winters)*

SLSF 34338; series 34000-34699
50-ton XM; 40'6" IL; 2933 cu. ft.
"AA" LOADING ONLY SEE INTERIOR STENCIL
▼ Beginning in 1955 the Frisco repaired and renumbered the remaining 1928 and 1930 GATC, PS or ACF boxcars from the 160000 to 163999 series. They were renumbered in a higher group due to retaining their wood sheathing when renewed. Number 34338 was captured in the CB&Q Hawthorne, IL yard in October 1960, with a fresh coat Frisco oxide red with the original paint scheme. *(Rail Data Services)*

SLSF 26044; series 26000-26215
55-ton XM; 40'6" IL; 3972 cu. ft.
▶ Between October and November of 1946 Pullman Co. delivered 300 forty-foot XMR 'Automobile' boxcars in series 154000-154299. They originally were equipped with two staggered Youngstown doors each side (covering fourteen-foot openings) and Evans type 'F' Auto Loaders for this service. Starting in January 1959 these cars had their loaders removed, increasing the overall cubic capacity from the original 3589 cubic feet. At the same time they were renumbered into the 153000 series. This de-equipping was in concert with the changes in finished automobile transportation with the coming of autoracks in 1960. An additional 92 boxcars were rebuilt and renumbered into the 16000-16152 series in the early-sixties. They were re-equipped with DF-2 Loaders and/or Belts and eight- or nine-foot doors by welding sheet steel over the left doors. The remaining boxcars Frisco performed minor repairs to the body, as well as removing the roof walks and renumbered into the 26000 series in 1970 and 1971. By the rebuilt dates Frisco had dropped the "SOUTHEAST…SOUTHWEST" from the "Ship It on the Frisco!" slogan. Our April 1971 rebuilt sample is spending its retirement in sunny Hugo, Oklahoma in 1984. *(Raymond F. Kucaba)*

SLSF 27154; series 27000-27299
55-ton XL, XM; 40'6" IL; 3854, 3903 cu. ft.

◀ The newly painted '2' indicates a renumbering after a full repaint from the 17000 to 17299 series. It was typical for Frisco to renumber by changing or adding the first digit or digits to the original numbers. Ordered between April and December 1948, they were the first PS-1 design boxcars produced for Frisco by Pullman-Standard. The first fifty (17000-17049) were equipped with D-F Evans Loaders and 8 full-length belt rails. Between 1969 and 1972 the Frisco reconditioned this group with the addition of strengthening gussets on either side of the door openings, but retained the eight-foot Superior panel doors. At the same time the roof walks were removed and the ladders were cut down accordingly. Note that the end roof panels have been replaced since these cars had no "bowtie" rib as built. Approximately 45 additional cars were renumbered in the mid-60's to the 111031-111112 series, these were for special Fish Meal service out of Mobile, AL. Number 27154 poses in the Sherman, Texas yard on November 30th 1980. *(Richard Yaremko)*

SLSF 27484; series 27300-27799
55-ton XM; 40'6" IL;
3903 cu. ft.

▶ This group of cars was built in March to June 1951 by Pullman-Standard numbered 17300 to 17799 series. The rebuilding and renumbering occurred between 1969 and 1972, usually being carried out at the large Springfield, Missouri shops. The rebuilding once again involved strengthening gussets to be added either side of the door openings and removal of the roof walks. Unlike the previous cars these rebuilds received a full repaint including the numbers. They were delivered with eight-foot Youngstown corrugated sliding doors. Ray found number 27484 in great condition on a siding in Galesburg, Illinois on July 26th, 1983. *(Raymond F. Kucaba)*

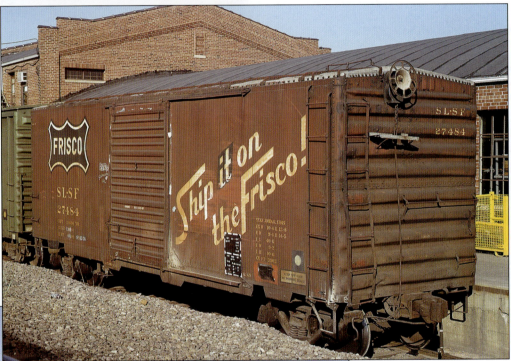

SLSF 17826;
series 17800-18049
55-ton XM;
40'6" IL; 3903 cu. ft.

◀ Notice the original applied classic "Southeast Frisco Fast Freight Southwest" slogan coming through the new paint. This group of 250 cars built by Pullman-Standard in December 1952, lot number 8046. Pullman-Standard received a lot of car orders from the Frisco due to being an on-line customer in Bessemer, Alabama. Pullman also used Frisco to deliver many new cars to other railroad customers west of the Mississippi. Bernie Wooller captured one example from the group in Huntsville, Alabama in May 1969. *(Bernie Wooller)*

SLSF 16402; series 16401-16403
55-ton XF; 40'6" IL; 3881 cu. ft.
WHEN EMPTY RETURN TO AGENT,
TRRA RY. ST. LOUIS, MO.

▲ This excellent down-on shot was taken in the BN Cicero, IL yard on the 4th of October 1977. The distinctive P-S roof has the signature bowtie formed on all of the panels. These three cars were rebuilt from a 500-car P-S order built between February and March 1954 (18050-18549). In March 1973 the Springfield shops altered these three by applying a special interior coating for Flour Loading (probably bagged on pallets) on the TRRA, which can be seen through the open Youngstown door. Part of the rebuilding included an additional plate below the doors, probably to allow the weight of forklifts with loaded pallets. *(Raymond F. Kucaba)*

SLSF 21083; series 21000-21099
55-ton XF; 40'6" IL; 3897 cu. ft.
ASSIGNED PROCESSED PACKAGED FOOD LOADING,
SL-SF MEMPHIS, TENN.

▼ The Frisco reconditioned more boxcars into food grade (XF) in 1974 (in the same fashion as #16402) for Kellogg assignment in Memphis, TN. They replaced 100 leased cars in the 15000-15099 series for the same service. Kellogg typically preferred forty-foot boxcars for their Memphis operations. The Springfield shops utilized 1954 built PS-1 boxcars from the 18050 to 18549 series as fodder for these rebuilds. The Kellogg business was important to the SL-SF and the road pulled other reconditioned XF boxcars from the 21500 series to keep numbers up for the service. The paint scheme remained Frisco oxide red with black background coonskins and "it", and some (like this example) received the large UP influenced reporting marks and numbers. Rolling by in Gaffney, South Carolina on January 27th, 1984. *(Paul Faulk)*

SLSF 18803; series 18550-19199
55-ton XM; 40'6" IL; 3897 cu. ft.

◄ In April and May 1956 P-S assembled these 650 general service boxcars at their Bessemer, Alabama plant. Number 18803 has retained its as-built paint scheme including the "SOUTHEAST…SOUTHWEST" part of the "Ship it on the Frisco!" slogan. The eight-foot Youngstown "47" sliding doors, roof walk and high ladders are intact even at this late date of March 8th 1980 in Fort Worth, Texas. This group of cars came equipped with P-S nailable steel floors, the first of many to come. The Frisco still had great use for many plain forty-foot general boxcars due to substantial freight forwarder traffic and being a major link between eastern and western railroads. Some of the freight forwarders the Frisco serviced were Western Carloading Co., Republic Carloading Co. and Acme Fast Freight. *(Richard Yaremko)*

SLSF 19292; series 19200-19899
55-ton XL (marked XM); 40'6" IL; 3897 cu. ft.
▲ Even though this boxcar is incorrectly marked XM, the larger DF-2 logo makes no mistake that it is equipped with Evans DF-2 loaders. Appliance loading was a typical assignment for these cars, considering the loaders, the eight-foot doors and (Stran Steel and Pullman) nailable steel floors. Pullman-Standard built these cars between August and September 1957 at their Bessemer plant. At least 113 cars had loaders installed starting sometime in the early sixties, the balance of cars in the group remained XM's. Note there is also a small ball and bar symbol on the door with a "DF" within. Appliance loads were common for either equipped or unequipped versions for this group. Whirlpool had a plant on-line in Fort Smith, AR, although this car was assigned to GE Appliance, KY on the Southern and L&N. This car sits white lined in Tulsa, Oklahoma on the 27th of October 1983. *(Richard Yaremko)*

SLSF 21519; series 21500-21666
55-ton XF; 40'6" IL; 3897 cu. ft.
▼ The demand for boxcars suitable for food products increased in the seventies. The Frisco reacted in 1977 by transforming 167 PS-1 XM boxcars from 1956 and 1957 orders, numbered between 18550 to 19899. The original and reconditioned cars were equipped with nailable steel floors and eight-foot Youngstown doors. The Frisco served a diverse customer base, including many food related shippers, so these XF's probably carried heavy bulk products like bagged flour or packaged foods. By the rebuilt date the Frisco simplified its paint scheme as a cost saving measure which included: the elimination of the black background from the coonskin and "it"; as well as an increase of the coonskin outline and the larger sans serif reporting marks and numbers. This overhead photo was taken overlooking the BN Cicero yard near Chicago in May 1981. *(Charles H. Zeiler)*

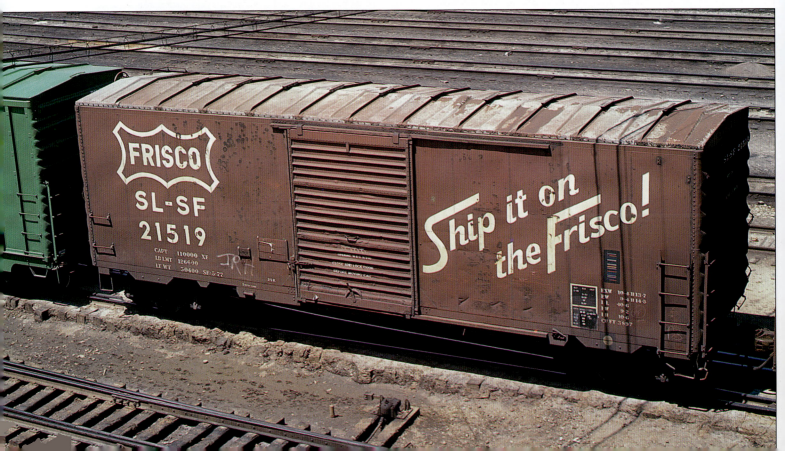

**SLSF 22063;
series 22000-22099 55-ton XM;
40'6" IL; 3897 cu. ft.**

▶ Frisco's Consolidated Mechanical Shop in Springfield rebuilt another 100 forty-footers as late as 1978, for general service. The crop for these came from the 19200 to 19899 boxcars built by Pullman-Standard in 1957. They retained their nailable steel floors, but most of them lost their eight-foot sliding Youngstown doors for Superior or fabricated doors. Our example demonstrates the simplified white only paint scheme. Dan Holbrook captured number 22063 just down the road on the BN in Eola, December 1984. *(Dan Holbrook)*

**SLSF 15097, 15096; series 15000-15099
55-ton XL; 40'6" IL; 3898 cu. ft. WHEN EMPTY
RETURN AGENT FRISCO RY. MEMPHIS TENN.**

▲ Between August and October 1967 the Frisco leased these Chicago Freight Car Co. rebuilt boxcars from unknown origins. During the sixties the Frisco used colors for their boxcars to signify specific assignments or equipment. The red-orange of this group signified assignment to Kellogg. Note the assignment stencil for Memphis the location of the Kellogg plant. The cars were specially equipped with DF-2 Evans loaders and belt rails. The nine-foot Youngstown exterior-post plug doors allowed a smooth interior surface to limit packaged cereal lading damage. Most, if not all cars had the pictured paint scheme, with no exclamation mark after the 'Ship it on the Frisco' slogan and black lettering. The October 14th, 1967 date and location of Chicago, Illinois of the photo would suggest they have just left the CFC plant. In 1969 Frisco leased another 75 cars of similar color, design and size from CFC, with the exception of having ten-foot Youngstown exterior post doors. The lease ended shortly after these cars were replaced by the 1974 rebuilt 21000 to 21099 XF boxcars. *(Owen Leander)*

**SLSF 16361; series 16354-16393
55-ton XL; 40'6" IL; 3903 cu. ft.
WHEN EMPTY RETURN TO FRISCO
RR. FORT SMITH, ARKANSAS**

◀ This series of boxcars was assigned to Whirlpool (ex-Norge Div. of Borg-Warner) in Fort Smith, Arkansas for refrigerators and freezers. Rebuilt in 1970 by Evans Products Co., originally from SL-SF 17300 to 18549 series Pullman-Standard forty-foot boxcars. It has been specially outfitted with Evans DF-2 19-belt rails (note the small DF-2 logo within the ball and bar symbol on the door) necessary to secure the high value lading. Gussets around the door opening have been added to deal with forklift weights when loading. Paul Winters caught our example soon after its rebuilding in 1971. *(Paul C. Winters)*

**SLSF 20404; series 20000-20424
55-ton XL; 40'6" IL; 3893 cu. ft.
WHEN EMPTY RETURN TO
A.T.N. R.Y. MOBILE, ALABAMA**

▶ In 1969 and 1970 Frisco leased 425 equipped forty-foot boxcars from Chicago Freight Car. Like the previous 'Kellogg' cars these were also equipped with DF-2 loaders and belt rails, except they had nine-foot Youngstown corrugated doors. These equipped cars were mostly assigned to specific shippers; a couple of examples were US Gypsum in Southard, Oklahoma and Scott Paper Co. in Mobile, Alabama. Note the Alabama, Tennessee & Northern assignment stencil, which was still a Frisco subsidiary till 1971. This car has a split personality with the traditional paint scheme of black background coonskin and serif reporting marks and number to the left of the door, and the white only "Ship it on the Frisco!" slogan to the right. Cicero, Illinois October 17th, 1977. (Raymond F. Kucaba)

50-Foot Boxcars

**SLSF 7088, 7064; series 7050-7099
55-ton XME, XML; 50'6" IL;
4772 cu. ft.; POOL 65
WHEN EMPTY RETURN TO
N&W RY. DETROIT MICH.**

▲▶ The favored Pullman-Standard was selected by Frisco to produce 100 cars in March 1954. The two groups were equipped with Evans DF loaders with 18 belt rails. They differed in that the first group (7000-7049) had seven-foot six-inch doors, while the second had an eight- and seven-foot staggered Youngstown doors. Some of the first fifty-foot PS-1's had riveted side panels like these cars. Our first example number 7088 is in its delivered scheme, and in auto parts service assigned to the Norfolk & Western in Detroit. While number 7064 is in front of the Irving, TX Frisco depot in July 1979 a month after it was repainted. It has still to receive its load limit and light weight stencil, but has received the then standard all white outline coonskin and 'Ship it…' slogan with a small "DF" logo near the left door. Note, that it also has received a Springfield shop special five-panel door.

(Jim Rogers collection) (Tony Lovasz)

SLSF 7702; series 7100-7799
55-ton XM; 50'6" IL; 4863 cu. ft.

▲ Frisco was impressed enough with the first fifty-foot PS-1's, so they placed an order for 700 more, although they were classified XM for general service. Pullman-Standard started building this lot from late in 1955 to February 1956. They were delivered with standard nine-foot Youngstown sliding doors, various makes of lading tie anchors, and Great Lakes Steel nailable steel floors. At least one car (#7365) in the order was converted with rooftop loading hatches before 1967. Richard found 7702 in its original paint scheme (although the white paint is streaking) in Bozeman, Montana on the 20th of September 1982. The original paint included the bars above and below the reporting marks and numbers and the distinctive safety dashes along the side sill. The Pullman builders logo is visible to the lower left of the door. With such a large series of cars it was inevitable that the Consolidated Mechanical Shop in Springfield reconditioned a majority of them. After reconditioning they were renumbered in the following series of boxcars (examples follow): 7840-7882, 7900-7906 series, 47000-47299 series, 177800-177823 series, 444000-444299 series. Interestingly, the seven cars in the 7900 series had 24" National cushioned sills applied sometime in the mid-60's, perhaps this was an experiment by Frisco to retrofit older fifty-footers.

(Richard Yaremko)

SLSF 7842; series 7840-7882
55-ton XML (later XL); 50'6" IL; 4863 cu. ft.;
POOL 176
WHEN EMPTY RETURN TO AGENT,
UP. RWY. COLUMBUS NEBR.

▼ Around 1966 the Frisco was in need of loader equipped non-cushioned boxcars, so they placed Evans DF loaders into boxcars on-hand. The cars they pulled from were the previously illustrated 7100 to 7799 from P-S built in 1956. They were re-numbered, it seems that the number '8' in 7842 has been re-stenciled over the original number. Frisco became more involved with pool cars for auto parts in the 1960's, this is one example captured in Tulsa on March 9th, 1984. Number 7842 was probably assigned to Douglas & Lomason Co. who manufactures automotive seat frames. There were three unusual cars in this group, 7857 to 7859 (ex-7150-7152 (IL 48'6" and 4671 cu. ft.)), which had ten-foot doors, 6" (B end) and 18" (A end) false bulkheads, and DF-2 loaders and nine belts for internal equipment.

(Ronald A. Plazzotta)

**SLSF 47219; series 47000-47299
55-ton XM; 50'6" IL; 4863 cu. ft.**

◀ By the late seventies the Frisco's Consolidated Mechanical Shops (CMS) in Springfield, Missouri had four production lines, three of them were for rebuilding cars. Between January and November of 1978 they were busy rebuilding these 300 cars from the 7100 to 7799 PS-1's from 1956. Most of the rebuilds received replacement nine-foot Frisco built 'Superior'-like five-panel doors, the minority had retained their Youngstown ones. They were equipped with nailable steel floors (note the graphic on the door) and lading tie anchors, so they were useful cars for general service. Fully dressed in the final all white lettering paint scheme recorded in Cicero, IL on the 4th of February 1981. *(Ronald A. Plazzotta)*

**SLSF 444240, 444259; series 444000-444299
55-ton XP; 50'6" IL; 4863 cu. ft.**

▲ This group was specially equipped for a specific commodity (XP), TIRES! They were refurbished with a Special Interior Coating while retaining their nailable floors and tie anchors for this specific service. They were loaded with other ladings (other than tires) needing clean interiors most typically paper rolls. Rebuilding was carried out the same time (throughout 1978) and from the same feedstock as the 47000 numbered rebuilds. Like the other rebuilds these cars remained non-cushioned and were constructed with either Youngstown or Frisco built panel doors. Frisco had two major tire manufacturers on-line: BF Goodrich in Miami, Oklahoma and Goodyear in Lawton, Oklahoma. The Goodyear plant started production in 1978, which more than likely was the impetus for the rebuilding of these cars. Illustrating the two door types on a clear 10th of December day in 1978 at the CNW Proviso yard, one can speculate they were on their way delivering tires to the Chrysler plant in Belvidere, IL. *(Ronald A. Plazzotta)*

**SLSF 154409;
series 154300-154439
55-ton XP; 50'6" IL; 4844 cu. ft.
WHEN EMPTY RETURN TO
AGENT, SL-SF RY.
SOUTHARD OKLA.**

▼Dan Holbrook captured number 154409 and his shadow in Havelock, Nebraska on August 21st, 1982. These 140 cars were ordered from Pullman-Standard in May 1957. They were originally equipped with type 'G' auto-loading racks for automobiles (AAR class XMR). By 1962 to the early '70's they had their racks removed becoming XM's. Starting around 1971 till 1978 thirty cars from the series had crane rails and belt rails fitted in the interior, classed XL and reduced cubic capacity (3896 cu. ft.). These thirty cars were renumbered into the 155000 series and were assigned to Mueller Brass in Fulton, MS (via Amory, MS) for outbound copper products. The remaining ninety boxcars were reclassified for special commodity loading (XP) in 1973. They received a 'Special Interior Coating' to handle gypsum/plaster (bagged) loading for US Gypsum in Southard, OK.

(Dan Holbrook)

SLSF 177813;
series 177806, 177807, 177812, 177813, 177819-177822
55-ton XML (later XL); 50'6" IL; 4863 cu. ft.

▲ These eight cars originally were built by Pullman-Standard in June of 1957 in the 7800 to 7839 series. They were equipped with eight-foot PS panel doors, P-S nailable steel floors and Evans DF loaders with 18 belt rails (7800-7805) or 9 belt rails (7806-7839). The eight cars represented by number 177813 were reconditioned and renumbered from the original series and some received the PS corrugated sliding door like this example. Note that the side sill 'fishbelly' is shallower than the 1956 order. Found in Tulsa, OK on the 9th of March 1984. Others from the 177800 series came from the 1956 P-S, 7100-7799 series. *(Ronald A. Plazzotta)*

SLSF 43542; series 43500-43699
55-ton XF; 50'6" IL; 4952 cu. ft.

▼ As the Frisco came into the sixties they continued to order from Pullman-Standard with 400 cars constructed in May 1960. This original order was numbered between 40000 and 40399 and they came with 15' 2" door openings closed with combination doors, the main one being an eight-foot Youngstown corrugated slider and an auxiliary Youngstown door making up the difference. Between October 1976 and May 1977 CMS had performed major surgery, by eliminating the plug doors (you can make out the riveted and welded patch), adding a unique ten-foot Frisco 4-panel door and roof walk removal. The rebuilds received new numbers, the later paint scheme, and were assigned for food service (XF). They retained their other equipment like: P-S nailable steel floors; Azee and MF Lock lading strap anchors; Equipco, National, Universal, and Ajax hand brakes. Rolling on the SP in San Luis Obispo, California on the 9th of October 1980. *(Peter Arnold)*

SLSF 40586; series 40500-40666
55-ton XM; 50'6" IL; 4952 cu. ft.

▶ These 167 boxcars came from the 40000 to 40399 series, P-S built in May 1960, that had combination sliding and plug doors. Again, in 1978 CMS in Springfield eliminated the plug doors and substituted a ten-foot Frisco 5-panel door (you can make out the patch replacing the plug door). The rebuilds received new numbers, the later paint scheme, and had their roof walk removed. They retained their other equipment like nailable steel floors, lading strap anchors, and various hand brakes. Superior, Wisconsin on the 22nd of June 1986. *(Roger Bee)*

SLSF 8051; series 8000-8149
70-ton XML (later XL); 50'6" IL; 4928 cu. ft.
WHEN EMPTY RETURN TO A.T.& N. R.Y. MOBILE, ALA.

▲ Cushioned boxcars on the Frisco were painted yellow, and they retained their yellow when repainted, unlike other colored cars. Starting with this group of boxcars built in February 1962, Frisco went to ACF (P-S competitor) for their cushioned boxcar purchase. Overall the features were ten-foot Superior seven-panel sliding doors, Waughmat type CG-5 Hydra-Cushion, 2 short Sparton belt rails, and lading strap anchors. Notably, there was one car with 9 full-length Sparton belts (#8112) and another six had 19 full-length DF-1 belt rails (8000-8002, 8084, 8120, 8138). The first 75 cars (like 8051) came equipped with: Apex running boards/ end steps, Timken roller bearings, Miner hand brakes, and Durawood flooring. Number 8051 was shot in its original all-black lettering paint scheme, which included a black background without white "…it…" in the "Ship it…" slogan, a HYDRA CUSHION logo, and white safety dashes on the side sill. Its assignment was probably Scott Paper in Mobile, Alabama. Saint Louis, Missouri sometime in February 1963. *(Paul C. Winters)*

SLSF 8129; series 8000-8149
70-ton XML (later XL); 50'6" IL;
◀ **4928 cu. ft.**

This is an example of the last 75 cars of the February 1962 ACF order. They were generally equipped with ten-foot Superior seven-panel doors, 20" Hydra-Cushion underframe, Sparton belt rails, and lading strap anchors. They differed with the following equipment: US Gypsum running boards/ end steps, Hyatt roller bearings, Peacock hand brakes, and Dowloc flooring. A great number of these boxcars when repaired and repainted in 1977 had their doors replaced with Frisco-built 4-panel sliding door. During repainting the 'HYDRA CUSHION' logo and black 'square' behind the "…it…" were dropped, as demonstrated by this nice overhead view of 8129 in Cicero, Illinois on June the 21st 1982.
(Charles H. Zeiler)

SLSF 8153; series 8150-8224
70-ton XML (later XL); 50'6" IL;
4735 cu. ft.
WHEN EMPTY RETURN TO G.T.W. R.R. BATTLE CREEK, MICH.

▶ The following year (1963) Frisco went back to ACF for another similar 75 cars built between April and November. The cars between 8150 and 8166 were equipped with Evans DF-B movable bulkheads (4928 cu. ft. (note the DFB logo near the side tack board)) while the remainder had Sparton 3-belt loaders. Some cars like 8153 came equipped with pallets. Otherwise they all were equipped with ten-foot Youngstown plug doors, Waugh Type 11-20" HYDRA CUSHION (note the cylinder hanging down in the center of the underframe), Durawood floors, US Gypsum running boards, Ellcon-National hand brakes, and McLean-Fogg floor clips. Tony Lovasz captured number 8153 in Irving, TX in October 1983 wearing the later yellow paint scheme, which included the large san serif reporting marks and numbers.
(Tony Lovasz)

SLSF 41035; series 41000-41199
50-ton XM; 50'6" IL; 4822 cu. ft.

▶ Frisco was in the market for more plain fifty–footers, so they turned to USRE to lease 200 cars that were rebuilt between July and December 1964 at their Blue Island, IL plant. The source of the original boxcars is unknown, but most have an original built date of 1937. Notice the extensive welded patches on the car sides, and the inspection door on the double-bar ten-foot Superior plug door (used for grain loading). These boxcars were non-cushioned and so received the boxcar red paint scheme without the "SOUTHEAST – SOUTHWEST". In July 1971 to February 1972 USRE rebuilt this series again, by replacing the plug door with a Superior 6-panel sliding door. They also received a spartan paint scheme that lacked the coonskin and "Ship it on the Frisco!" slogan. Found on a day in November 1964 Fort Worth, Texas.
(K. B. King Jr., Richard Yaremko collection)

SLSF 8383; series 8325-8424
70-ton XML (later XL); 50'6" IL; 4953 cu. ft.
WHEN EMPTY RETURN TO A.T.& N. AGENT MOBILE, ALA.
▲ A second order was received from General American Transportation Co. in April to May 1965, the first being in February and March 1964 (8225-8324). The differences being a straight side sill, an unusual ten-foot five-inch Superior plug doors, Equipco hand brakes and Keystone 20" cushioning applied to the first order, whilst the second were equipped with ten-foot Youngstown plug doors, Miner hand brakes and 20" HYDRA CUSHION underframe. Common equipment between the orders was Evans DF-2 loaders, Durawood floors and lading strap anchors. Assignment for number 8383 is probably for Scott Paper in Mobile, Alabama. Recently repainted with an incorrect built date, but retaining the "CUSHIONED CAR" lettering, poses in Columbus, OH in April 1968.
(Paul C. Winters)

SLSF 8619; series 8425-8624
77-ton XML (later XL); 50'6" IL; 4950 cu. ft.
▼ The Frisco returned to ACF for an additional 200 cars delivered in early 1966. Exterior features included ten-foot Youngstown plug doors, 20" Keystone end-of-car cushioning, Ureco hand brake, and Apex running boards. They were originally outfitted with Transco "Sparton" SEL 3 full-length belt rails (4931 cu. ft.). Number 8619 must have had different fittings accounting for the larger cubic capacity of 4950. The plug doors created a smooth interior along with Durawood floors, Azee lading strap anchors and McLean-Fogg floor clips were ideal and typically loaded with paper products or wood products. These yellow Frisco boxcars could be seen anywhere in North America, this one in San Luis Obispo, CA on November 16th, 1980. *(Peter Arnold)*

SLSF 8790; series 8625-8824, 8825-8874
77-ton XL; 50'6" IL; 4950 cu. ft.

▲ Subsequent ACF lot numbers 11-06144 and 11-06145 were built from February 1968. On the exterior both of these lots were exactly the same, but they varied in interior equipment. Although there are always exceptions like this example, during repainting and repairing in 1977 the original ten-foot Youngstown plug door has been replaced with an exterior post Youngstown plug door. One of the distinctive exterior details was the ACF "Precision Design" stiffener impressions to the right of the door opening. Both lots were delivered without running boards, with 20" Keystone end-of-car-cushioning and McLean-Fogg floor clips. The first 200 cars were delivered with Evans DF-2 belt rails and Azee lading anchors, indicated by the two symbols on the doors, whilst the remaining 50 cars had their interior cubic capacity reduced to 4920 due to Evans sidewall fillers and load dividers. In Fort Worth, TX on March 9th, 1980. *(Richard Yaremko)*

SLSF 10292; series 10000-10299
77-ton XL; 50'6" IL; 4950 cu. ft.
WHEN EMPTY RETURN AGENT SL-SF RY. CO., CANTONMENT, FLA.

▼ Clean, classic, and cushioned Frisco yellow paint scheme, in Belen, New Mexico on a sunny day in August 1970. The ACF St. Louis plant built these 300 cushioned boxcars in February and March of 1969. Like the previous 1968 order they came equipped with 20" Keystone cushioning, ten-foot Youngstown plug doors, Azee lading anchors, Ajax handbrakes, and Evans DF-2 belt rails. With all these interior fittings it's no wonder they were assigned heavily for paper-based products, this one in particular assigned to the large St. Regis paper mill on-line in Cantonment, Florida. There is just enough road grime to clearly define the "Precision Design" stiffening impressions. *(K. B. King Jr., Richard Yaremko collection)*

**SLSF 15504; series 15500-15574
55-ton XL; 50'6" IL; 4828 cu. ft.
WHEN EMPTY RETURN
AGENT FRISCO RY
MEMPHIS, TENN.**

▶ In March 1969 SLSF leased these 75 cars from Chicago Freight Car (CFC), it seems they were rebuilt by stretching forty-foot boxcars. As per the orange 'Kellogg' cars these blue cars received the same lettering "CFC" paint scheme without the exclamation mark '!' on the end of the 'Ship it on the Frisco' slogan. Perhaps the blue signified an assignment to General Foods in Memphis, the same blue was applied to EL insulated boxcars for the same service. They were equipped with ten-foot Youngstown plug doors and Evans DF-2 belt rails. Note that as delivered these boxcars did not receive running boards. *(Ronald A. Plazzotta)*

**SLSF 12107; series 12000-12199
77-ton XL; 50'6" IL; 4952 cu. ft.
WHEN EMPTY RETURN TO
AGENT FRISCO RAILWAY
MACMILLAN ALABAMA**

◀ You can almost smell the paint of this car as seen outside of the Pullman-Standard Bessemer, Alabama in February 1970. Not following convention this group originally received yellow even though they were NOT cushioned. Frisco went back to Pullman after a decade absence of fifty-foot boxcar orders, atypically without cushioning unlike the previous ACF orders, although they were equipped with ten-foot Youngstown plug doors, Evans DF-2 loader belts, Azee lading anchors, M-F style G floor clips, and Ajax hand brakes. The cars were assigned to the very important customer MacMillan-Bloedel in Macmillan, AL for paper or plywood/particleboard loads. *(Jim Gibson)*

**SLSF 12117; series 12000-12199
77-ton XL; 50'6" IL; 4952 cu. ft.**

▼ During 1976 most if not all of the boxcars in this group received non-cushioned boxcar red paint with the "early" all white lettering, with serif (railroad roman) reporting marks and numbers. At the same time most of them had their doors replaced with exterior post Youngstown plug doors, but retained the same equipment listed for the yellow number 12107. The first ten cars of the series, 12000 to 12009, had their cubic capacity reduced to 4655 cubic feet due to the inclusion of Evans Air-Pac moveable bulkheads and pallets. Dan Holbrook was able to capture number 12117 in boxcar red in the BN Eola yard on January the 18th, 1983. *(Dan Holbrook)*

SLSF 13043; series 13000-13299
77-ton XL; 50'6" IL; 5267 cu. ft.
"WHEN EMPTY RETURN TO AGENT, M. & B. RAILROAD, NAHEOLA, ALABAMA."

▲ At first glance these look like standard P-S fifty-footers, but note the extra space between the two welded end stampings. This has increased the internal height to 11' 2" making these boxcars EXCEED Plate C. As seen outside the Pullman-Standard Bessemer plant in the original gray paint scheme, complete with white background coonskin. The built dates for these 300 boxcars were between July and August 1970. The gray paint signified paper products service, and one of the major assignments was to James River Paper Co. in Naheola, AL on the Meridian & Bigbee. The markings on the ten-foot Youngstown plug doors illustrate the main interior equipment, lading anchors (Azee) and DF-2 belt rails *(Jim Gibson)*

SLSF 13163; series 13000-13299
77-ton XL; 50'6" IL; 5267 cu. ft.
WHEN EMPTY RETURN TO AGENT FRISCO R.R. MAC MILLAN, ALABAMA

▼ Inevitably the delivery 1970 gray paint gave way to boxcar red in the middle of 1976. The paint scheme used was the "early" all white scheme with the reporting marks and numbers in a serif font. During this time most but not all cars had their doors replaced with exterior post Youngstown plugs, whilst retaining all of the other equipment. A majority of boxcars in this group were assigned like this one, to MacMillan-Bloedel on-line Macmillan, Alabama for paper rolls. This photo on October 28th, 1981 in Aurora, Illinois highlights the extra height these cars had compared to the standard height Frisco boxcars either side. *(Dan Holbrook)*

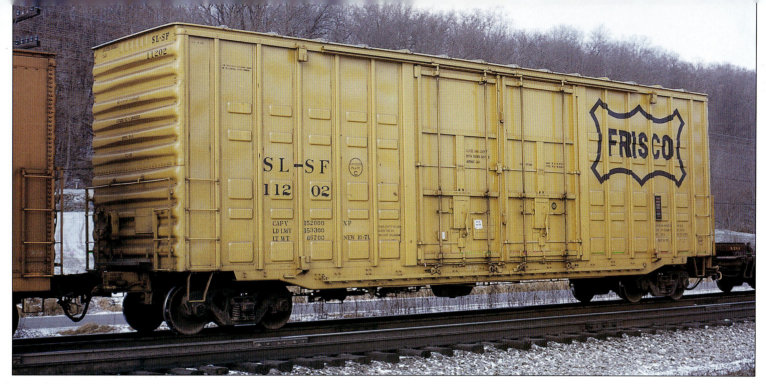

SLSF 11202; series 11000-11249
76-ton XP; 50'6" IL; 6150 cu. ft.
WHEN EMPTY RETURN AGENT TOE RY. VALLIANT, OKLAHOMA
▲ Between October and November 1971 Frisco went back to ACF to construct 250 special service (XP) boxcars. These cars were the first time SL-SF received boxcars with waffle sides. They also had a "high-cube" interior height of 12' 10" (stenciled with an EXCEED Plate C) with a pair of exterior post 8' 0" (wide) by 11' 11" (high) Youngstown plug doors. Following convention these cars were painted yellow with only an extra large coonskin and cushioned with ACF's 20" FREIGHT-SAVER. Other equipment included Azee lading anchors, Durawood floors, Morton end platforms, and Ajax hand brakes. Notice that ACF utilized P-S ends and roof, instead of the customary Stanray components. These cars were purchased for paper loading from the Weyerhaeuser Co. plant in Valliant, Oklahoma. *(Rail Data Service)*

SLSF 42149; series 42000-42099, 42100-42499
77-ton XM; 50'6" IL; 5080 cu. ft.
▼ By the time 1972 came around Frisco needed some clean new non-cushioned, "free-runner" general service boxcars. They took delivery of 500 ACF built cars throughout 1972 in two orders, the first 100 in February and the next order in October and November. ACF was able to use Stanray ends and roof for these plain vanilla Plate B boxcars as demonstrated by Mr. Zeiler's excellent overhead shot at BN's Cicero yard in 1981. They were delivered with ten-foot Youngstown corrugated sliding doors, lading anchors and E. L. Bruce's Durawood floors. All exterior-post boxcars only came with only coonskins, this one with a black background coonskin. *(Charles H. Zieler)*

SLSF 43039; series 43000-43199
55-ton XM; 50'6" IL; 4288 cu. ft.
▲ Frisco once again augmented their boxcar purchases with 200 leased cars from USRE. Between August and October 1972 the Atlanta, Georgia plant of Southern Iron and Equipment Co., an Evans subsidiary, stretched these former forty-foot PS-1 boxcars to fifty-footers. They replaced the roofs with Stanray versions and added ten-foot Youngstown sliding doors and their characteristic welded drop straight sill with triangular door opening gussets. Note the roller bearings in the solid bearing cast truck frames on this 13th of August 1984 in Superior, Wisconsin. *(Roger Bee)*

SLSF 11967; series 11900-11984
76-ton XP; 50'6" IL; 6175 cu. ft.
WHEN EMPTY RETURN TO AGENT SL-SF RY. FT. SMITH ARK.
▼ These "high-cube" waffled boxcars were specifically purchased for Whirlpool fridges or freezers from their Fort Smith, Arkansas plant (ex-Norge division of Borg-Warner 1966). American Car & Foundry built 85 cars in May 1974 with the same basic carbody as the double-plug door version, except with a single ten-foot six-inch Youngstown sliding door and a straight side sill. With these new high-cubes Frisco was able to offer Whirlpool two high stacking of full-size fridges and to complement the assigned 16000 series forty-footers. Irving, Texas in June 1983.
(Tony Lovasz)

SLSF 11284;
series 11250-11299
76-ton XP; 50'6" IL;
6175 cu. ft.
▼ In August 1974 Frisco went back to ACF to order another 50 "high-cube" boxcars to the same design as the 11000 to 11249 series. The main difference this time around was Stanray was able to supply the ends and roof. These yellow boxcars differed with a stenciling of ACF FREIGHT-SAVER-20B advertising the cushioning used, whilst not stenciling their special assigned service. Missouri Pacific and Texas, Oklahoma and Eastern had identical boxcars that were part of a pool assigned to Weyerhaeuser Co. This shot clearly shows the uneven sizes and patterns of the waffles as car 11284 rolls-by in San Luis Obispo, California on September 10th, 1981. *(Peter Arnold)*

**SLSF 44024;
series 44000-44299
77-ton XM; 50'6" IL;
5277 cu. ft.**

▶ Pullman-Standard's Bessemer plant produced these 300 cars in September and October 1974. Even though they were classified as XM plain boxcars they came equipped with ten-foot P-S corrugated sliding doors, nailable steel floors and lading band anchors. Like the other exterior-post boxcars, these also came with only large coonskins (black background), but unlike the similar ACF boxcars from 1972 this group had a plate C clearance. Peter Arnold had his camera ready in Las Vegas, Nevada on the 16th of July 1977.
(Peter Arnold)

**SLSF 13568; series 13500-13599
77-ton XL; 50'6" IL; 5277 cu. ft.**

▲ During the same period of construction of the previous series, the Bessemer plant was busily constructing 100 loader-equipped boxcars completed in September 1974. The outward appearance differed with the application of a flat P-S roof and even waffles. The open door allows us to see the four rows of belt rails built into the waffles, which allowed the interior cubic capacity to remain the same as the 44000 to 44299 series. Besides the loaders this group was otherwise equipped with same doors, floor and anchors. Illuminated by a western sun in Sacramento, California on April 9th, 1981.
(Peter Arnold)

**SLSF 11313;
series 11300-11324
77-ton XL; 50'6" IL;
6150 cu. ft.**

◀ Another Peter Arnold photograph this time an overhead view in Colton, CA on May 12th, 1983. By the time ACF finished building these 25 high-cube paper cars in February 1976, the ends had been changed to a non-terminating style. The overhead shot clearly shows the riveted flat Stanray roof. Other features were the two eight-foot Youngstown plug doors per side and ACF FREIGHT-SAVER-20B cushioned underframe. Interior equipment consisted of lading band anchors and laminated wood floors. Even though there is no assignment stencil these were probably also in the Weyerhaeuser pool, along with identical cars for Mopac and TO&E. *(Peter Arnold)*

60-Foot Boxcars

SLSF 9016; series 9000-9024
87.5-ton XAP (later XP); 60'9" IL; 5991 cu. ft.

▲ The first purchase of sixty-foot boxcars of course would come from Frisco's favored Pullman-Standard in September and October 1963. P-S placed their HYDROFRAME-40 cushioned underframe throughout the series. Other exterior features were a pair of eight-foot Camel plug doors, plain sheet roof panels, Miner hand brakes, Apex running boards, and Timken roller bearings in ASF trucks. Although yellow was correctly used for these cushioned cars, the application of covered hopper style "FRISCO" was non-standard for boxcars. This series of boxcars were mainly in auto parts service, probably Ford. It's in Eola, Illinois on October 18 1982. *(Dan Holbrook)*

SLSF 9204; series 9200-9205
90-ton XML (later XL); 60'9" IL; 5880 cu. ft.

▼ The first and only Evans sixty-foot boxcars were these six cars built in July 1967. One can make out the 20" HYDRA-CUSHION cylinder hanging in the middle of the car. Evans was able to install their 19 belt Damage Free (DF) loaders in their own plate C car design. The doors were eight-foot Superior six-panel sliding types, and additional equipment included Miner handbrakes and 2 1/4" laminated Durawood flooring from E.L. Bruce. Number 9204 demonstrates the repainted scheme with large sans serif marks and numbers, thicker coonskin outline, and black "it", as it sits in La Crosse, Wisconsin on the 27th of October 1985. *(Roger Bee)*

SLSF 9027; series 9026-9035
81.5-ton XL; 60'9" IL; 5880 cu. ft. POOL 608
WHEN EMPTY RETURN TO AGENT
L&N R.R. NASHVILLE

▲ These sixty-footers were assigned to Ford glass service on the L&N in Nashville. Frisco purchased this group from Thrall in February 1969. Note the double seem weld lines outlining the inner posts and the in-step on either side of the eight-foot Youngstown plug doors. Interior appliances to safeguard the lading are: Evans 9-belt rails, Armco floors, Equipco moveable bulkheads and floor keepers, and HD-FR 15 FreightMaster cushioning. BN yard Eola, IL March 13th 1982. *(Dan Holbrook)*

SLSF 9307; series 9300-9314
91.5-ton XP; 60'9" IL; 5880 cu. ft. WHEN EMPTY
RETURN AGENT SCL RWY. FERNANDINA, FLA.

▼ Along with SCL and L&N, Frisco ordered this pool of boxcars from the Bessemer plant of Pullman-Standard in January 1975. The pool was assigned for paper loading to Container Corporation of America in Fernandina, Florida. The Frisco's cars came equipped with ten-foot Youngstown plug doors, 15-inch FreightMaster cushioning and lading tie anchors (most probably in the waffle indents). Here we witness number 9307 in its original paint scheme with a relatively small coonskin in San Luis Obispo, CA on July the 25th 1986.

(Peter Arnold)

86-Foot Boxcars

SLSF 9100; series 9100-9109
50-ton XML (later XL); 86'6" IL; 10000 cu. ft.

▲ The Frisco was heavily involved with the auto industry either through on-line auto plants and parts suppliers or as an important bridge route between east, west and mid west auto facilities. It was no surprise the railroad supplied pool cars for auto stampings like this first 86-footer built by Thrall Car Co. in 1964. They were delivered with four aluminum ten-foot Youngstown plug doors and were left natural, although after repainting like our example the doors were painted silver. Other equipment was Keystone 20 hydraulic cushioning and Equipco load dividers (5-full length belts). We find the class car in Tulsa, Oklahoma on March 9th 1984 with a late spartan paint. In 1965 an additional ten were ordered from Thrall in the following series 9110 to 9119. *(Ronald A. Plazzotta)*

SLSF 9126; series 9120-9133
72-ton XL; 86'6" IL; 10000 cu. ft.
POOL BRO

▲ This group of boxcars was built at Pullman's Bessemer plant between November 1967 and January 1968. As of this photo taken in Irving, Texas on September 27th 1981, it has been assigned to BRO, Brownstown, Michigan after many black patches. P-S installed a Hydroframe-40 for cushioning and P-S rub rails. Number 9126 still sports its original paint scheme complete with "CUSHIONED CAR", "Ship it on the Frisco!" and the PRR car code of "X-60G". *(Richard Yaremko)*

SLSF 9136; series 9134-9138
72-ton XL; 86'6" IL; 10000 cu. ft.

▼ Dan Holbrook shot 9136 in Eola yard on the BN in October 1985 still in its as delivered paint, albeit with patch paint and some modern day graffiti. This lot and the following lot (9139-9147) both built by Greenville Steel Car in October 1969 and March 1970 respectively. This group had 20-inch travel ACF cushioning and Evans load dividers and bulkheads, whilst the following group had 20-inch Keystone cushioning and Equipco load dividers and bulkheads.

(Dan Holbrook)

Stock Cars

**SLSF 47420; series 47200-47699
40-ton SM; 39'9" IL; 2600 cu. ft.**

▶ This is a rare photo of a Frisco stockcar and the oldest freight car in the book, initially built in 1910 and 1911 by ACF's Terre Haute, IN plant. The Frisco started rebuilding these cars in 1943; our example has been rebuilt in August 1956, almost two years prior to this photo being taken in March 1958. The cars had a steel underframe and framing, wooden tongue and groove roof, and a rebuilt wooden door with metal hardware. A typical coon-skin herald and reporting marks were placed on wooden slats on the left side between posts. At least 30 of these stockcars lasted on the roster until 1960, plus an additional 250 of a larger 3153 cu. ft. design.

(K. B. King Jr., Dick Kuelbs collection)

Refrigerator Cars

**SLSF 333008; series 333000-333049
82.5-ton RPL; 51'0" IL; 4270 cu. ft.**

◀ The Frisco handled a lot of Pacific Fruit Express, Santa Fe, Fruit Growers Express and Western Fruit Express mechanical reefers in bridge traffic. It wasn't until May 1971 they had FGE's Alexandria, VA plant construct fifty mechanical reefers to serve their region. The reefers were copies of the FGE standard, assembled using Berwick underframes, and Youngstown sides and ten-foot six-inch plug doors. They were equipped with York refrigeration units powered by Emerson power units. Other features included 20-inch Keystone end-of-car cushioning and 2-piece Equipco load dividers. Paul Faulk was on-hand in Spencer, North Carolina on the 2nd of November 1975.

(Paul Faulk)

**SLSF 222016;
series 222000-222049
62.5-ton RPL; 51'0" IL;
4270 cu. ft.**

▶ Four months later, in September 1971, another fifty cars arrived from Fruit Growers Express. The significant difference between the orders was internal this series came equipped with 2-piece load dividers from Evans Products. For an unknown reason this group also had a lower tonnage rating. This excellent angle shows the other side of these reefers, clearly highlighting the screened doors providing access to the York-Emerson refrigeration-power combination. Ferris, Texas on March 15th 1980.

(Richard Yaremko)

Insulated Boxcars

GARX 50579; leased from series GARX 100-53999
48.5-ton RBL; 50'1" IL;
▶ **4360 cu. ft.**

The Frisco and its subsidiaries were major players for bridge traffic between eastern and western railroads. One of the subsidiaries that connected to the Santa Fe and a short route to the west coast was the Quanah, Acme & Pacific Railway Co. Here is an example of the 'Quanah Route' "The Transcontinental Cut-off" in June 1957, complete with a specially designed "Quanah Route" coonskin. The QA&P railroad leased these insulated boxcars from General American Car Co., built by the lessor in March 1957. Besides the insulation the car featured "No Damage" nine row loading devices in the walls, seven-foot seven-inch insulated Youngstown plug doors and Duryea underframes.
(Jim Rogers collection)

SLSF 6093; series 6000-6099
70-ton XLI (ex-RBL); 50'1" IL;
4430 cu. ft.

◀ The SL-SF serviced a diverse region with many food related customers and eventually Frisco purchased insulated boxcars for this type of service. ACF built 100 such boxcars in June and July 1961 and they came painted in freight car red with the "Ship it…" slogan and the additional advertising of "LOADER EQUIPPED INSULATED…CUSHIONED". These cars predated the use of yellow for cushioned boxcars. The loaders were nine-belt Sparton brand and the cushioning was Barber tube-type from Stanray. Other features included nine-foot Youngstown/Camel plug doors, Doweloc floors, Ajax handbrakes, and US Gypsum running boards. Frisco preferred using the class "XLI" for its insulated boxcars, recently over-painted "RBL" in LaGrange, IL on May 24th 1979.
(Raymond F. Kucaba)

SLSF 46027;
series 46019-46093
74-ton XLI
(marked XL);
50'1" IL; 4430 cu. ft.

▶ In 1980 the Springfield shop started reconditioning the previous ACF 1961 built XLI's. Typically they also were renumbered by adding a "4" digit. The shop repaired rusted body panels and removed the running boards. Note that insulated boxcars usually have an overhanging roof, in this case a Stanray roof. The reporting marks and numbers were repainted larger and in a sans serif typeface. Richard found this one in Great Falls, Montana on April's fool day in 1987. *(Richard Yaremko)*

NIRX 14003;
series 14001-14085
70-ton RBL; 50'1" IL;
4618 cu. ft.

▶ Frisco leased eighty-five insulated boxcars from North American Car Corporation, which also built the cars. It was common at the time for the lessee to have their own paint scheme applied to the cars. This group was painted the newly adopted (February 1962) yellow scheme for cushioned boxcars HYDRA-CUSHION is the type of cushioned underframe, which is clearly seen. Initially the cars came with NIRX reporting marks but they eventually received SL-SF marks and retained the original numbers. These cars were fitted with ten-foot Superior plug doors and DF bulkheads and side fillers to tightly secure the lading, but later some received pallets. Dick found our example on the Rock Island in Dallas on the 13th of October 1963. *(Dick Kuelbs)*

SLSF 6145; series 6100-6164
70-ton XLI (ex-RBL); 50'1" IL;
4281 cu. ft. WHEN EMPTY RETURN TO AGENT SL-SF R.R. PARIS, TEXAS

◀ One of Frisco's most valued customers was Campbell Soup in Paris, Texas, so it's no surprise that many new insulated boxcars were assigned to them to protect that service (some from this series). General American delivered these cars to the railroad in September of 1963, equipped with Keystone 20 cushioned underframes and 23-inch center-offset ten-foot, six-inch Camel plug doors. Other typical equipment for cars in canned goods service was the use of Evans DF-B bulkhead loaders and side fillers. Interestingly they were constructed with aluminum roofs in an attempt to reduce the lightweight of the cars. Around 1972 three cars had heater hooks installed, numbers 6108, 6126 and 6138. Found in an excellent repaint yellow scheme in Denison, TX on November 30, 1980. *(Richard Yaremko)*

SLSF 6178; series 6165-6264
70-ton XLI; 50'1" IL; 4281 cu. ft.
WHEN EMPTY RETURN TO AGENT SL-SF R.R. PARIS, TEXAS

▶ These Frisco insulated boxcars were a signature car for the railroad and could be seen all around the country, here is one in Grand Forks in July 1983. This is another General American XLI purchased in February 1964 and also assigned to Campbell Soup. Notice that this car, like others, has had a stencil applied near the door stating that the floor is equipped for 55,000-pound axle loading enough for a forklift with a pallet load. It's easy to pick a repaint job if the "it" in "Ship it…" has no black background square. Unlike the previous order these came with galvanized steel diagonal-panel Stanray overhanging roofs. Although they're equipped the same with Evans DF bulkheads and side fillers, Youngstown ten-foot six-inch plug doors (this series had them centered with the car side), 20-inch Keystone cushioned underframe, Equipco handbrakes, and combination "Durawood" (center) and oak floors from E.L. Bruce Co. (ends). *(Peter Arnold)*

**SLSF 6382;
series 6265-6414
70-ton RBL (later XLI);
50'1" IL; 4281 cu. ft.
WHEN EMPTY RETURN
TO AGENT SL-SF R.R.
MEMPHIS, TENN.**

◄ Dan Holbrook was able to capture number 6382 in its original paint scheme with the black background square behind the white "it" in Eola, IL on January 18th, 1983. This series of 150 insulated boxcars came from General American in May of 1965. The major external difference from the previous GATC offerings is the fishbelly side sill; other minor changes were full-length "Durawood" floors and Ureco handbrakes. Even though many cars from this series were also dedicated to "soup service", this example is assigned to one of the Memphis customers, perhaps Hunt Foods, Ralston Purina, Allied Mills, A. E. Staley, General Foods, or Schlitz. *(Dan Holbrook)*

**SLSF 14127; series 14100-14128
70-ton RBL; 50'1" IL; 4565 cu. ft. WHEN EMPTY RETURN TO
AGENT N & W R.R. CO. ST. LOUIS, MO.**

▲ The Frisco leased these RBL's specifically for a particular shipper on the N&W in the Saint Louis area. These exterior-post insulated boxcars were built in October 1965 and received the typical yellow paint scheme for a cushioned boxcar. The builder and lessor for these cars is North American Car Corporation and they featured a whopping twelve-foot wide door the largest single door width the Frisco rostered. The twenty-nine cars were equipped with 20-inch cushioned underframe, side fillers and DF-B bulkheads. Number 14127 sits on SP rails in Dallas, Texas on December 12th 1965. *(Dick Kuelbs)*

**SLSF 6503; series 6415-6514
70-ton RBL; 50'1" IL; 4600 cu. ft.**

▼ The legendary photographer K.B. King was handy in Fort Worth Texas in May 1977 to capture this sample of an Evans insulated boxcar. There is an assignment stenciled on the car side although it's not legible, but one thing is for certain, this is a non-standard repaint, observe the non-italic "CUSHIONED CAR". Evans Products Co. built them in July 1966 using their propriety DF-B bulkhead load dividers and side fillers along with a Superior ten-foot six-inch plug door and 20-inch Hydra-Cushion underframe. These were the first insulated boxcars not to receive running boards, however they still received high-mounted brake wheels. *(K. B. King Jr., Richard Yaremko collection)*

SLSF 6607; series 6515-6664
70-ton XLI; 50'1" IL; 4640 cu. ft.
WHEN EMPTY RETURN TO AGENT SL-SF R.R. HUGO, OKLA.
▲ The following year (1967) Evans provided Frisco with 150 more XLI's in the month of October. This group of insulated cars are identical to the preceding Evans group except for the Youngstown 10' 6" insulated plug doors and Evans one-piece bulkheads. The floor insulation was 3.5" styro-foam from Dow while the rest of the car was fiberglass. Even though it was to be returned to the SL-SF agent in Hugo it's ultimate destination was the Campbell Soup plant in Paris, Texas. The silhouette of the HYDRA-CUSHION cylinder can be made below the center of the car in Irving, Texas on 27 September 1981.
(Ronald A. Plazzotta)

SLSF 6698, 6729; series 6665-6764
70-ton XLI; 50'1" IL; 4333 cu. ft.
▶▼Frisco went back to General American for 100 insulated cars between January and February 1968. Both have their original paint schemes intact although number 6729 has Cots stencils and ACI label (now painted over) added. If you look carefully the GATX builders mark can be made out on the lower right of the sill. Typically for SL-SF XLI's they were equipped with Evans side fillers and load dividers, Superior 10-foot 6-inch insulated plug doors, and 20-inch cushioning (in this case Keystone). The first example is found in Huntsville, AL September 1968 whilst the second was captured on the west coast in San Luis Obispo, CA again in September 19 1981.
(Bernie Wooller) (Peter Arnold)

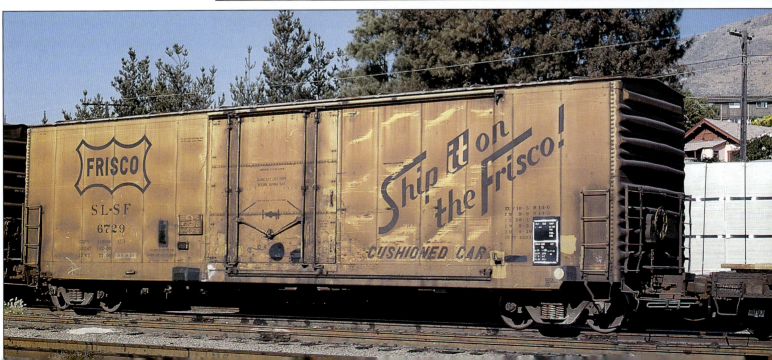

**SLSF 9502; series 9500-9510
80-ton XLI; 60'1" IL; 5371 cu. ft.
WHEN EMPTY RETURN TO AGENT FRISCO, SHERMAN, TEXAS**

▶ The first foray by Pullman-Standard into insulated boxcars for the Frisco were these sixty-footers constructed in June 1968. They were equipped with 20-inch Keystone cushioning, Evans side fillers and bulkheads, Youngstown ten-foot, six-inch exterior-post plug doors and Miner handbrakes. This example was found in Toledo, OH on June 12th 1979 in the original paint scheme with the covered hopper billboard "FRISCO" with a minute "CUSHIONED CAR" under the "S". Perhaps the whole series were assigned to Johnson & Johnson for medical products. *(Raymond F. Kucaba)*

**SLSF 9513; series 9511-9514
82-ton XLI (marked XL); 60'1" IL; 5409 cu. ft.**

▲ Here is another example of the June 1968 Pullman-Standard-built insulated boxcar. For some reason this car has been stenciled to a higher cubic capacity and incorrectly stenciled as an "XL". One thing is known this is a repaint job, notice that the reporting marks and numbers are large and in a "UP like" sans serif font. The difference between the two series under the same lot order is the cushioning; this series had 20-inch Cargo-Cushion type. During the repaint the assignment stencil was painted over, but one can speculate that it was still in Johnson & Johnson service since its laying-over in the Sherman, Texas yard in 30 November 1980.

(Richard Yaremko)

**SLSF 6889; series 6842-6912
70-ton XLI; 50'1" IL; 4360 cu. ft.
WHEN MTY RET. TO AGT. CNW BLUE EARTH, MINN.**

▼ Ironically, Green Giant had a cannery in Blue Earth and Frisco assigned a yellow insulated boxcar. This series of boxcars arrived on the property in May of 1971 from ACF, and also a previous 1969 order, series 6765 to 6841 and 6977 to 6999. Distinctive external features include the ACF Precision Design indents to the right of the door opening combined with a ten-foot, six-inch insulated Youngstown plug doors. Other equipment common on these insulated cars SA-20 Keystone cushioning, Evans side wall fillers, Evans non-swivel bulkheads, Miner handbrakes and Bruce 2.25-inch hardwood floors. In West Chicago, IL on September 28 1985. *(Dan Holbrook)*

SLSF 6958; series 6948-6976
70-ton XLI; 50'1" IL; 4400 cu. ft. WHEN EMPTY RETURN TO AGENT N&W RR. ST. LOUIS, MO.

▲ ACF in May 1971 delivered this group, almost identical to the previous lot, in fact they were only one lot number apart, #11-06218 and #11-06219 (this series). The only differences between the orders were the increase of the cubic capacity due to the use of Evans Air-Pak bulkheads. The Precision Design impressions still remained and gave strength to the car sides when the doors were opened. The actual customer is not known for this car, but what is known is that Frisco insulated cars did haul a variety of commodities like chemicals, silica and paper, besides beer, canned goods and food stuffs. Jim Eager was lucky to find this original Frisco yellow paint scheme in 1987. Take particular note of the "AIR PAK" logo to the left of the door and above the tack board. *(Jim Eager)*

SLSF 600023; series 600000-600264
68-ton XLI; 51'6" IL; 4829 cu. ft. WHEN EMPTY RETURN AGENT SL-SF RY. MEMPHIS, TENNESSEE

▼ Later in 1971, in the months of November and December, SL-SF tried Pacific Car & Foundry for a 165 order of insulated boxcars. They came with a PCF roof, exterior-posts and Stanray end, equipped with 20-inch Keystone cushioned underframes, Preco bulkheads, and ten-foot six-inch exterior-post Youngstown plug doors. They were delivered in this unique beige body with an oversized black outline coonskin with a white background. The significance of beige was to mimic the typical contents hauled, beer from the Schlitz brewery in Memphis, which opened on-line with an American Can facility in 1972. Frisco was a great promoter of industries on-line and ahead of the game when ordering these cars for the service. Here is an excellent shot of one of these insulated cars in train in Georgetown, Louisiana on March the 19th of 1975. *(Raymond F. Kucaba)*

**SLSF 700000; series 700000-700099
68-ton XLI; 51'6" IL; 4856 cu. ft.
WHEN EMPTY RETURN AGENT SL-SF RY.
MEMPHIS, TENNESSEE**
▲ A lot of beer must have been flowing from Schlitz for Frisco to order another 100 almost identical RBL's delivered in February 1973. PCF constructed an additional identical (with the first PCF series) 100 cars in July 1974, numbered in the 600165 to 600243. The difference between the 600000 series cars and these was internal with the use of Preco bulkheads with Air Bags. The class car was snapped in Cicero, Illinois on December 22nd, 1984 dressed in the same paint scheme as the previous series. Although the assignment for these insulated boxcars was for beer, they would on occasion haul other commodities like canned foods, paper and plastic bags. *(Raymond F. Kucaba)*

**SLSF 700267; series 700100-700299
70-ton XLI; 53'4" IL; 5159 cu. ft.**
▼ The last insulated boxcars the Frisco purchased were these 200 cars from Pacific Car & Foundry in August and September 1977. The interior length of this series was increased therefore the increase in cubic capacity. A major exterior difference was the elimination of the outside posts replaced by lap riveted side panels. Even though they retained their beige color the Frisco coonskin was positioned to the left of the door, only a black outline and was sized similar to the yellow RBL's. The reporting marks and numbers were increased in size and boldness, but they retained the same font. These cars were seen and can still be seen all across the country and especially memorable due to this unique paint scheme. The use of exterior post Youngstown ten-foot six-inch doors, PCF roofs and Stanray ends was standard across SL-SF PCF insulated boxcars. It was not surprising to find number 700267 in the BN Eola yard in Illinois on December 14, 1984. *(Dan Holbrook)*

Flat Cars and Bulkhead Flats

**SLSF 4058; series 4052-4061
50-ton FMS; 44'4" IL;
WHEN EMPTY RETURN TO VALIANT, OKLA.**

◄ SL-SF altered this series of bulkhead flatcars in 1956 from flatcars built from March to June in 1930 by VB&I Co. The Frisco shops fabricated new bulkheads and riveted them to the original carbody. Probably most of this small series of rebuilds were assigned to Dierks Forest, Wright City, OK (hardboard), interchange at Valliant, OK (note that Valliant has been incorrectly spelt when stenciled on the car). A few years earlier in 1952 another series (4000-4045) were also altered the same way but intended for wallboard service. Here we see number 4058 loaded with hardboard in the PRR Columbus, OH Grandview yard in January 1963.
(Paul C. Winters)

**SLSF 3900; series 3900
125-ton FD; 57'9" and 21'0" flat IL;**

► The Frisco only had one depressed center flat car and we see it on the Lehigh Valley, Sayre, PA in May 1974. The Springfield shops built this flat in kit form in the second quarter of 1953. General Steel Casting supplied the underframe, truck frames, truck bolsters and center plate. The Universal drop staff handbrake is in the up position at the other end of the car. This flatcar could negotiate a 19 degree curve when coupled, but was able negotiate a 38 degree curve when uncoupled, note the extra large poling pockets for that purpose.
(Rail Data Services)

**SLSF 2152;
series 2100-2199
55-ton FM; 53'6" IL;**

◄ In November 1957 Frisco built 100 general-purpose flatcars using a GSC underframe as a base. From 1958 to 1961 a little less than half of the cars had GSC bulkheads applied with an interior length of 48 feet 6 inches. They all came equipped with Superior hand brakes, although the general-purpose ones were of the drop staff style. These were very versatile flatcars for the Frisco, they could handle loads of steel, pipe, wallboard, lumber and utility poles as seen here in Springfield, MO in January 1994. *(Charles H. Zeiler)*

SLSF 5636; series 5600-5649 70-ton FMS (some later FBS); 48'6" IL;

▶ As the usefulness of the recently converted flatcars to bulkhead flats was realized, Frisco ordered an additional fifty cars. However, this time they were purchased assembled by General Steel Industries (named change from General Steel Casting) receiving them in August and September 1963. Approximately 13 cars from the series were equipped with lockers at the A end, possibly in dedicated wallboard service. Here is an example of a perfectly loaded bulkhead flat with Brandon tie-downs with chains and Dierks Forest wrapped hardboard load in Huntsville, Alabama. Notice the trough above the reporting marks, which held the tie-downs where a couple can be seen. *(Bernie Wooller)*

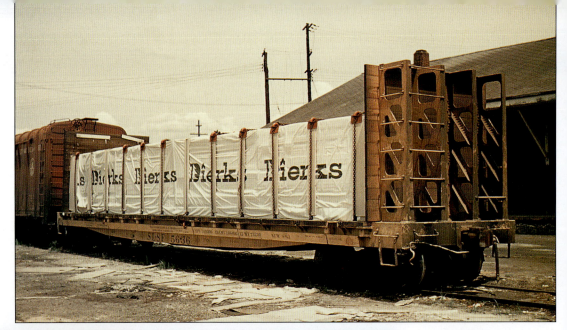

SLSF 5688; series 5650-5699 70-ton FMS (some later FB); 48'6" IL;

◀ For a change here is an example of an unloaded bulkhead flat to better see the details, in train in San Luis Obispo, California on the 11th of August 1981. Again, Frisco shops assembled these fifty bulkheads from GSI kits in April 1964. The cast steel underframes were well liked by Frisco because they were almost indestructible. Cars numbered 5650-5659 came equipped with Brandon tie-downs, and they all received "Peacock" Ellcon-National handbrakes. *(Peter Arnold)*

SLSF 4109; series 4100-4149 85-ton FBS; 70'0" IL;

▶ Frisco handled a significant amount of cast iron and steel pipe loads mainly from the Birmingham, Alabama area, with on-line customers like American Cast Iron Pipe Co., US Pipe & Foundry Co. and Consolidated Pipe and Supply Co. To service this traffic the railroad ordered specially designed bulkhead flatcars built by Ortner in March 1966. They were equipped with 15" FreightMaster end-of-car cushioning, Brandon load binders and Ureco handbrakes. You can make out chains and tie-downs in the nearly full-length trough on the outside of the side sill. Considering it is February 1983 the yellow paint had held up well when Dan Holbrook captured number 4109 in the BN Eola yard. *(Dan Holbrook)*

SLSF 3806; series 3806-3807
57-ton FMS; 59'6" IL;
▲ ◀ Here are two views of one of two August 1968-built Thrall special flatcars. The canopies cover aircraft parts at this time coming from the Wichita, Kansas area, the location of these photos in April 1989. Due to its location the car was probably used in Boeing service to Renton, Washington. The underframe was equipped with a HD-15E FreightMaster cushioning device to safeguard the high value cargo. The original color for the flatcar was yellow, while the original canopy color is unknown. *(both, Jim Kinkaid)*

SLSF 4184; series 4150-4199
87.5-ton FBS; 70'0" IL;
▼ This is a follow-up fifty-car order from Ortner Car Co. arriving on the property in 1971. They were the same overall design and utilized the same 15" travel FreightMaster cushioning. The differences from the 1966 order was the lack of the chain trough, the chain assemblies and tie-downs came from MacLean-Fogg, and the handbrakes were supplied by Ellcon. Besides pipe loads seventy-foot bulkheads could be utilized for lumber service like this example in Eola, IL on March the 17th 1983. They were also ideal for other on-line customers like stainless steel vessel manufacturer Paul Mueller Co. from Springfield, MO. *(Dan Holbrook)*

Wood Racks

SLSF 5106; series 5000-5199
55-ton LP; 38'3" IL; 3620 cu. ft.

▲ Like other southeastern railroads, Frisco called their pulpwood cars wood racks. This series of wood racks were assembled by the Yale Tennessee shops starting late 1951 and into 1952, utilizing grated sloped floor cast steel underframes from GSC. The whole series was leased to the Central of Georgia in the early sixties and renumbered into the 15000 to 15199 series. By mid-1967 they were returned at which time Frisco added 24" extensions to the end bulkheads (total IH 9'0") making these "shorties" more useful. In the late seventies the Frisco was gradually renumbering their wood racks, (most became 4300-4499 or 35000-35199) so they wouldn't mix with 5000 series bulkhead flats. Number 5106 is found with its welded extensions in the TASD interchange yard in Mobile, Alabama on May the first 1977. *(Nicholas J. Molo collection)*

SLSF 4555; series 4500-4749
77-ton LP; 45'3" IL; 4038 cu. ft.

▼ The cast steel frames made these cars survivors considering the beating they receive during loading and unloading. The author was surprised when I found Frisco yellow 4555 sitting in the ex-RIP tracks of the Amory yard on the morning of June 9th 1990. These 250 wood racks were renumbered in 1979 from 5300 to 5449 series built in April 1956, and from 5450 to 5549 series built in March 1957, by the Yale shops. Nearly every siding on the Southern Division (east of Memphis) had wood rack loading yards, servicing the many pulp, paper and plywood mills in the area, including Scott Paper in Mobile, Gulf States in Green Tree, AL, MacMillan Bloedel Ltd. in Macmillan, AL, Alabama River Pulp Co. in Fountain, AL, and St. Regis Paper Co. in Cantonment, FL. *(Nicholas J. Molo)*

SLSF 555796; series 555000-555799
70-ton FMS; 49'1" IL; 4946 cu. ft.

◀ By 1979 Springfield converted at least 75 bulkhead flatcars from the 2000-2199 series (built in 1956 and 1957) to wood rack service. The conversions entailed removing all the wood from the deck and bulkheads and welding a fabricated sloped floor with drainage slots in the center of the deck. They were renumbered into the 555000-series, avoiding any number conflicts with other wood racks or bulkhead flats. This group was assigned almost exclusively on the branch lines in southern Oklahoma and Arkansas (the other major pulp and paper region on the Frisco) that possibly serviced Weyerhaeuser and Georgia Pacific plants in those states. Fully loaded number 555796 was found working on the Kiamichi Railroad in Hugo, OK on October 14th, 1988. *(Raymond F. Kucaba)*

FRISCO Equipped and Unequipped Gondola Cars FRISCO

SLSF 61676; series 61600-61899
77-ton GB; 52'6" IL; 1745 cu. ft.

▲ It's hard to believe but the body paint is freight car red, the original freight car red applied in November 1953 by Pullman-Standard following a "Greenville" design. The previous two almost identical orders were instead painted all black although used the same lettering diagram, 61000-61399 blt. March to May 1949 and 61400-61599 blt. April 1953. They all came equipped with steel floors and P-S ends doors with Wine door balancer and locks. All handbrakes were of the lever style although the first and last orders used Klasing brand and the middle order had Universal. The first series were easy to spot because they had side hold down clips on the side sheets, whereas the following orders cam with Wine lading band anchors on the top coping. Number 61676 is being loaded with scrap tin in Rochelle, IL on 24 March 1981.
(Dan Holbrook)

SLSF 51537;
series 51000-51899
77-ton GB; 52'6" IL;
1745 cu. ft.

▶ General unequipped gondolas are one of the most abused freight cars. So, it's not surprising that in the early seventies the Frisco rebuilt the previously featured P-S gondolas. These rebuilds included welding the ends closed, replace side panels, and repainted with the large "FRISCO" billboard in white between the ribs. Otherwise they retained all their previous features shown by this shot of number 51537 on October 20th, 1983 in Eola, Illinois.
(Dan Holbrook)

SLSF 70211;
series 70050-70249
77-ton GB; 65'6" IL;
1777 cu. ft.

◀ Frisco only rostered 250 sixty five-foot six-inch gondolas, the first fifty delivered in December 1948, series 70000 to 70049 (the recommended AAR design built by Pressed Steel Car Co.). The remaining 200 gons like our sample in Eola in 1983 were built in April to June 1956, came from Frisco's favored Pullman-Standard. The P-S gondolas came with steel floors, Wine end door locks, Wine lading band anchors and Klasing handbrakes. These features along with its length resulted in great utility for Frisco, which served many on-line steel makers, steel fabricators and pipe manufacturers. Dan Holbrook captured number 70211 in his favorite haunt Eola yard on February 13th 1983. *(Dan Holbrook)*

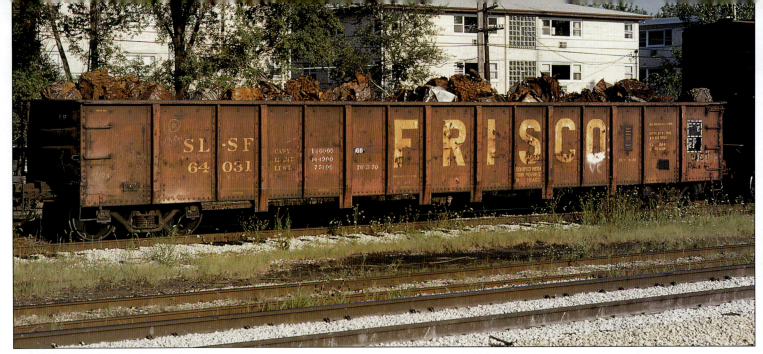

SLSF 64031; series 64000-64039
70-ton GB (ex-GBR); 52'6" IL; 2328 cu. ft.

▲ Between September and November 1957 the Frisco purchased 400 gondolas from Pullman-Standard, originally featuring lading band anchors on the top chord. Even though our example is marked GB by this 1985 August day in La Grange, Illinois. Around 1962 the lading anchors were not present to accommodate a roof, classed GBR and as the stenciling states "EQUIPPED WITH FOUR MOVEABLE BULKHEADS". The car was wood lined, had fixed ends, and Equipco handbrake, but at one time it had a three-piece sectional Stanray roof with Apex running boards. The roof was to protect their usual loads, steel products like steel plate, while the moveable bulkheads would in this case protect the car from damage not the load. The six ribs extending below the side sill are unique to these gons and possibly a Frisco only feature. *(Raymond F. Kucaba)*

SLSF 63008; series 63000-63014
70-ton GBS; 52'6" IL; 4977 cu. ft.
FOR SCRAP AUTO BODY LOADING ONLY
WHEN EMPTY RETURN TO SL-SF ANY JUNCTION

▼ In 1966 Frisco selected fifteen gondolas from the 400 1957 P-S gons and extended the sides for scrap auto body loading. They renumbered the fifteen to separate them from the general-purpose gondolas. Interestingly the shop forces decided to raise the position of the Equipco handbrakes on the extension, likewise with the large billboard "FRISCO". The last revenue car in the train is passing by Sherman, Texas on October 23 1983, probably heading to or from the Arlington GM auto plant. *(Richard Yaremko)*

**SLSF 65003; series 65000-65099
95-ton GBS (later GB);
52'6" IL; 2327 cu. ft.**

▶ In February 1966 Darby, (a new manufacturer for Frisco) delivered 100 specially equipped gondolas (GBS). The special equipment is one full length Transco SL-2 belt rail each side. This excellent interior shot in Reading, PA 1993, shows the belt rail just below the top channel on the opposite side. The belts perhaps retained tarps to cover the lead or copper or zinc concentrates from the "Lead Belt" in Missouri (the state produces 60 percent of the nation's supply of lead). Note the straps over the fixed end ribs to strengthen the ends from being typically deformed, and also the alternating thin and thick ribs on the car sides. The first half of the order had steel floors (like this car) while the second came lined with wood.
(Craig T. Bossler)

**SLSF 63501;
series 63500-63502
90-ton GBS; 52'1" IL;
3207 cu. ft.**

◀ Three gondolas from the previously mentioned Darby series (built February 1966) were converted in September 1972 for specialized service. The conversion involved increasing the sides and ends by two-feet and the addition of 9 DF belt rails for the full length of the interior of the sides. The note in the equipment register describes the service was for "Electrodes". One of these gons was in transit in McCook, Illinois on May 24th, 1982.
(Dan Holbrook)

**SLSF 69017; series 69010-69019
87.5-ton GBS; 51'10" IL; 2319 cu. ft.
WHEN EMPTY RETURN TO SL-SF
RY. AT NEAREST JUNCTION
AAR CSD145**

▶ Frisco was hot for gondola orders and tried St. Louis Car Co. in September 1967 with an order for 200 gons, numbered in the 65100 to 65299 series. Like the preceding Darby order this group also received one Transco SL-2 loader rail and lading band anchors, in later years the rails were de-activated and the gons became GB's. Just after delivery Frisco shops converted the first ten from the series for maximum 84-inch diameter steel coil service. This involved the addition of full-length cradles on the floors with four moveable bulkheads, FreightMaster end-of-car cushioning, telescoping roof sections, and removal of the lading anchors. By the time Dick Kuelbs shot this one on September 4 1977 in Irving, TX the roof sections were gone, although the end plates (note the vent) and sliding roof channel (on the top of the side coping) remain.
(Dick Kuelbs)

**SLSF 69013;
series 69010-69019
87.5-ton GBSR;
51'10" IL; 2319 cu. ft.
WHEN EMPTY RETURN
TO SL-SF RY. AT NEAREST
JUNCTION AAR CSD145**

◀ This is another example of the 1966 built St. Louis Car gondolas that were converted to haul coils. Number 69013 was again converted by Springfield in 1977, but his time all the end plates and side channels were removed to accept yellow fiberglass covers. These fiberglass covers were tested and proved successful on gondolas in the 64000 to 65059 series. Ten cars from the 64040 to 64059 series transferred their covers to the 69010-69019 series in 1977 demonstrated here by the cover number 64050. In March 1984 in Irving, Texas. *(Tony Lovasz)*

**SLSF 65497; series 65300-65499
97.5-ton GB (ex-GBS); 52'6" IL; 2327 cu. ft.
ASSIGNED LEAD SERVICE BUICK-HERCULANEUM**

▲ Frisco ordered another 200 specially equipped gondolas in January 1968 from Greenville Steel Car of Pennsylvania. The equipment fitted consisted of Evans DF-2 belts, Wine A-2 Cont. lading anchors, and Ajax handbrakes on a body with a steel floor and fixed ends. Around 1972 the belt rails were de-activated and the gondolas were re-classified as GB's. All the ribs have the same cross-section, unlike the St. Louis Car uneven rib design. We see an example of one of these cars in Irving, Texas on a day in May 1977. It also has an assignment recently stenciled on the second panel from the left. The assignment "BUICK-HERCULANEUM" was for St. Joe Lead Company that had mines near Buick, MO and a smelter in Herculaneum, MO. The Frisco collected the traffic on the Salem Branch, hauled it to Lindenwood (St. Louis), and then forwarded it down the River Division to Crystal City for interchange with the MoPac. Interestingly, the smelter at Herculaneum had rotary dumpers set-up for dumping standard gondolas. *(Lynn Savage)*

**SLSF 65534; series 65500-65599
97.5-ton GB; 52'6" IL;
2327 cu. ft.**

◀ As per other gondolas recently acquired, this group was equipped with Transco belt rails. These must have not been used because in the early seventies the cars were classified for general service. The uneven alternating ribs and short angular bottom cut-offs are distinctively St. Louis Car Company design features. By the built date of January to March 1969 St. Louis Car had become the St. Louis plant of General Steel Industries (GSI). GSI's influence was felt in this production with the use of cast steel underframe ends supplied by GSI. Other features of these gondolas were Wine lading and angle band anchors, Schaefer roping staples and Ajax handbrakes. The large billboard paint has held-up well for this 1986 shot in the BN Eola yard in Illinois. *(Dan Holbrook)*

SLSF 65906; series 65750-65949
97.5-ton GBS (later GB); 52'6" IL; 2328 cu. ft.

▲ Although this gondola has uneven alternating side ribs they are straight for their full height, a spotting feature of Darby built gondolas. Darby built these 200 gons in July 1971, interestingly with Stanray fixed ends differing from the first Darby order. Typical for Frisco of the period, they came equipped with Evans DF belt rails, Wine lading and angle band anchors, and Schaefer roping staples. The original paint has fully survived till this 9th day of December in 1982 in Eola. *(Dan Holbrook)*

SLSF 66083; series 66000-66199
98.5-ton GB; 52'6" IL; 2244 cu. ft.

▼ Pullman-Standard won over Frisco in September 1975 with these 200 GB gondolas. One can speculate how they won them over but it could have been the all riveted body compared to all of the competitors. This was an attractive feature due to easy replacement of damaged side panels, which was a common occurrence for general service gons. These Pullman gondolas were all steel construction including the fixed non-terminating ends with an Ajax handbrake. Richard Yaremko caught number 66083 loaded with metal shavings in Irving, TX on the 6th of December 1980.

(Richard Yaremko)

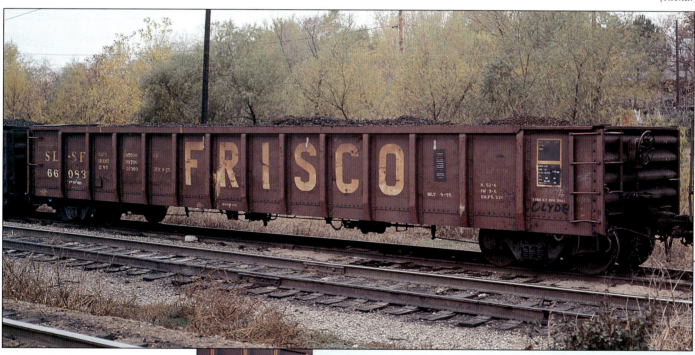

SLSF 69060; series 69050-69074
98-ton GBSR; 48'0" IL;
2024 cu. ft.

▶ By September 1975 Frisco was comfortable enough to purchase the single purpose USRE built coiled steel gondolas. The cars basically had a trough floor covered with steel fabricated covers place on a HYDRA-CUSHION underframe. The total carbody and frame was coated in Frisco red with white sans serif lettering, while the covers received railroad roman (serif) "FRISCO" on the side panels only. There is known to be at least one set of covers which have white outlined coonskins. Rolling in April 1981, Irving Texas. *(Tony Lovasz)*

SLSF 69075; series 69075-69079
98-ton GBSR; 48'0" IL; 2024 cu. ft.

▶ When Frisco ordered an additional five coil steel cars in November 1976, they came totally painted in black with white lettering. This time the covers didn't receive the "FRISCO" on the sides, but managed to retain the end panel SL-SF lettering. Both orders had Morton step tread surrounding the sides and ends of the body, not to mention the cushioned underframe. Here we find a slightly weathered example of the black scheme in Portland, Oregon on July 31 1983.
(Peter Arnold)

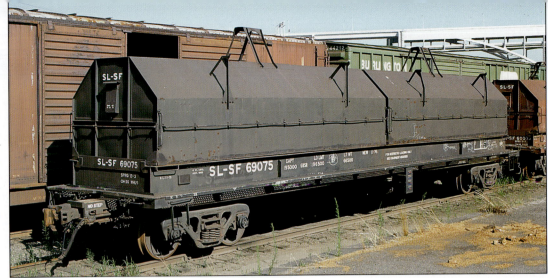

 Open Hoppers  Two-Bay Hoppers

SLSF 90941; series 90800-91599
55-ton HM; 33'0" IL; 2145 cu. ft.

▲ Frisco received 2,900 1935 AAR standard twin offset hoppers constructed in several orders from 1948 to 1957. Our example is from the largest order of 800 hoppers built in May 1949 by Pullman-Standard. Three hundred cars from the first order were built by Mt. Vernon Car Co. (90500-90799) exactly one year earlier. One series of 500 hoppers (90000-90499) built in July 1948 were delivered with notched angular ends. The Frisco utilized these cars for many types of loads and some survived up to merger date in 1980. At some stage all these hoppers received the large black background coonskin (seen here January 1968), although a few repaints in the seventies received just white outlined coonskins. *(Paul C. Winters)*

SLSF 92293; series 92100-92399
55-ton HM; 33'0" IL; 2145 cu. ft.

▼ Our second example of twin-offset hoppers was from the series ordered in April to June 1954 from the P-S Bessemer plant. All of these Frisco hoppers received Ajax handbrakes and Enterprise Type D door locks. Typical ladings for these hoppers on the Frisco were coal (steam and metallurgical), coke, gypsum rock, ores, sand and aggregates. Portage, Wisconsin October 1969. *(Rail Data Services)*

Three-Bay Ore Hoppers

SLSF 80122; series 80000-80199
100-ton GSS; 29'8" IL; 1629 cu. ft.

▲ Along with the Southern, L&N and GM&O, Frisco purchased identical P-S ore hoppers in February and March 1954. All four railroads were involved with hauling South American iron ore from the port of Mobile to the steel mills in Birmingham. A unique construction feature was the end "troughs" beyond the main hopper compartments. Notice that the ore didn't usually fill the capacity of the hoppers, and that it also had a distinct red coloring. The hoppers were equipped with Wine door locks and Miner hand brakes. Howard Robins was able to capture two of the cars entering in East Thomas yard into Birmingham, May 1974. *(Howard L. Robins)*

SLSF 180002; series 180000-180199
100-ton HTS; 29'8" IL; 1629 cu. ft.

▼ By 1979 the Frisco renumbered the hoppers to avoid conflicts with covered hopper series above and below. They were also reclassified into HTS (special purpose hoppers) and repainted with new sans serif reporting marks and numbers. By this July 26th 1983 photograph on the BN in Beardstown, Illinois, they were hauling taconite from the Missabe Range. Taconite is a pellet mixture of iron ore and lime fluxing material and is therefore lighter than the higher concentrate ore, allowing fuller use of the hopper capacity. The Frisco used these ore hoppers for their intended service until 1980, although they probably carried other high-density commodities. *(Raymond F. Kucaba)*

Three-Bay Open Hoppers

SLSF 87267; series 87200-87299
100-ton HT; 49'6" IL; 3407 cu. ft.

▶ Between April 1964 and January 1968 Pullman-Standard's Bessemer plant produced 400 hoppers for the Frisco. Number 87267 is an example of one order built in May 1967, seen freshly painted outside the Bessemer plant tracks. The main reason for three-bay hopper purchases was for coal service, although gypsum rock was another common lading. Note the contrast of the boxcar red body and black hoppers and trucks. All of the P-S three-bays had Wine door locks, but the handbrakes were a mixture of Miner and Ajax.
(Jim Gibson)

SLSF 87445; series 87400-87599
100-ton HT; 45'1" IL; 3420 cu. ft.

▲ The Frisco served two coal regions, the larger in northern Alabama and the other straddling eastern Kansas, northeast Oklahoma extending to Arkansas. These regions were producing more and more metallurgic and steaming coal as the seventies came around. Frisco reacted by purchasing two orders from Greenville for 400 hoppers, this series in October 1972 and a following series (87600-87799) in September 1975. At this point hoppers were still being painted into boxcar red and carried the large white billboard "FRISCO". Lynn Savage has captured this hopper loaded with black diamonds in Irving, TX on February 1st 1981. *(Lynn Savage)*

SLSF 88228; series 88200-88399
100-ton HT; 45'0" IL; 3433 cu. ft.

▼ The Consolidated Mechanical Shops (CMS) in Springfield were no strangers to high-quality production line work of many types of new cars for the Frisco. So, therefore starting in February 1976 CMS built five orders of 1380 hoppers till June 1978. These hoppers were constructed using ACF kits. Note the small coonskin with "BUILT BY FRISCO" inside of it, near the dimensional data panel. All of the Frisco built hoppers were painted black and received the Futura Black typeface in white. This group of two hundred hoppers was built between January and May 1977. Irving, TX, February 1st 1981. *(Lynn Savage)*

**SLSF 88470;
series 88400-88599
100-ton HT; 45'0" IL;
3433 cu. ft.**

▶ The Springfield shops completed these 200 cars from ACF kits July to December 1977. These were identical to the previous orders except that the reporting marks and numbers were changed to sans serif lettering. Like all the previous three-bay hoppers they came equipped with Wine door locks. This is what 100 tons of coal looks like heaped the length of the car in Irving, Texas in 1981. *(Lynn Savage)*

Woodchip Hoppers

**SLSF 5809; series 5800-5819
70-ton HTS; 50'9" IL; 5400 cu. ft.**

▲ The first woodchip hoppers Frisco owned were standard three-bay hoppers with extended side rebuilt in 1960. Frisco got serious two years later purchasing Ortner built woodchip hoppers in March 1962. These extra tall hoppers stood 15-feet 3-inch from the railhead. The four-bays used Wine door locks and the hand brakes were Universal. Ortner was able to keep the interior free of vertical posts by using channels on the exterior car body. Here we see loaded number 5809 going over the hump at Tennessee yard in Memphis in 1980. *(Nicholas J. Molo collection)*

**SLSF 93137; series 93100-93154
92.5-ton HTS; 66'7" IL; 6940 cu. ft.**

▼ Woodchips became more in demand for use at paper and chipboard mills in the late sixties. Frisco wanted to increase the tonnage able to be carried with this lightweight commodity, so in March to April 1967 (93000-93029) and February 1968 (93030-93054) received 55 woodchip hoppers from the Ortner Freight Car Company. The hopper door locks were Wine (favored by the Frisco) and the handbrakes were Equipco or Ajax. These 66-foot behemoths had six hoppers and were mainly used on the Southern Division. In 1978 both series were reconditioned, repainted, and renumbered as we see here in Amory, Mississippi on the 22nd of April 1980.

(Nicholas J. Molo collection)

FRISCO Covered Hoppers

Two-Bay Covered Hoppers

SLSF 83703; series 83650-83849
77-ton LO; 29'3" IL; 1958 cu. ft.

▶ The Frisco received nearly 500 identical covered hoppers built by three builders from 1945 to 1950. Number 83703 comes from a group of hoppers constructed by Mount Vernon Car Co. in July and August 1948. They featured eight-rectangular loading hatches, Enterprise outlet doors, and Ajax handbrakes. Originally covered hoppers were painted black and received a small white outline coonskin placed between the ribs. Later they were repainted into a body color of grey and received a large billboard "FRISCO" and black lettering as seen in October 1977. *(Paul C. Winters)*

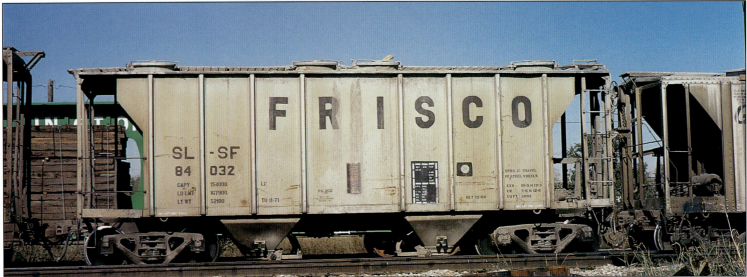

SLSF 84032; series 84000-84099
77-ton LO; 29'3" IL; 2003 cu. ft.

▲ Pullman-Standard's Butler, PA plant built 100 PS-2 covered hoppers from December 1958 to January 1959. The Frisco served many cement and silica customers and these covered hoppers were ideal for these commodities, especially the eight 30-inch circular loading hatches that sealed the compartments from moisture. P-S manufactured the four discharge gates, hoppers and vibrator castings, while purchasing the Universal handbrakes and Apex running boards. This is an example of one of these cars with the original small billboard "FRISCO" found in Irving, Texas in April 1984. *(Tony Lovasz)*

SLSF 84178; series 84100-84199
77-ton LO; 29'3" IL; 2010 cu. ft.

▼ In November 1959 SL-SF received 100 of this follow-up PS-2 design, where the width was widened by inches to increase the cubic foot capacity by seven. As intended by Pullman this car is hauling cement, notice the small spill between the center 30-inch diameter hatches. Besides the same Pullman proprietary gates, hopper doors and vibrator castings as the last series, these came with Miner D-3290-XL hand brakes. This example is under a cloudless sky on March 30, 1982 in Tulsa, Oklahoma that happens to be the place it was last re-weighed. *(Ronald A. Plazzotta)*

**SLSF 85238;
series 85150-85299
100-ton LO; 36'11" IL;
3010 cu. ft.**

▶ Frisco management allowed more than five years to elapse before ordering more two-bays. The favored Pullman-Standard delivered 150 covered hoppers in February 1966. They were fitted with US Gypsum running boards and steps, Klasing hand brakes (high-mounted), and Wine discharge gates. Richard captured one of these high cubic capacity hoppers wearing its original paint scheme in Sherman, Texas on the 30th of November 1980. *(Richard Yaremko)*

**SLSF 85302;
series 85300-85399
100-ton LO; 36'11" IL;
3010 cu. ft.**

◀ In November 1968 Pullman-Standard built another one hundred 3,010 cubic foot covered hoppers. This series and the previous 1966 series received US Gypsum running boards. This group was also the first of this design to receive low-mounted hand brakes. In 1979 some were reconditioned by Springfield at which time received the large sans serif reporting marks and numbers like this example. Eola, Illinois February 26, 1982.
(Dan Holbrook)

**SLSF 78193;
series 78000-78199
100-ton LO; 36'11" IL;
3010 cu. ft.**

▶ Between October and November 1972 Pullman-Standard constructed another two hundred covered hoppers identical to the 1966 and 1968 groups. Frisco purchased this type of hopper to mainly service silica sand deposits in south central Oklahoma. The sand was used for glass making, foundry sand and roofing granules to name a few. It seems as though the hopper bays below the side sill have been painted black. Jim Eager was close to home in Toronto, Ontario when his keen eye came across this original painted gem in December 1984. *(Jim Eager)*

SLSF 78595; series 78500-78749
100-ton LO; 37'11" IL; "2971" TYPE, 2970 cu. ft.

▲ Frisco eventually ordered from ACF, receiving 250 two-bay covered hoppers built at their Huntington plant in February 1975. The CF-2971 type Center-Flow design was built to Plate B clearances and had extended non-cushioned draft gear, these were the major differences from the standard 2970 design. The hoppers featured four 30-inch diameter hatches along the roof centerline and two center discharge gravity outlets. Like the P-S cars these mainly hauled silica sand, but probably cement and chemicals as well later on. The hoppers below the side sill were painted black originally as seen on this February 1976 day in Irving, TX. *(Lynn Savage)*

SLSF 78209; series 78200-78399
100-ton LO; 36'11" IL; 2980 cu. ft.

▼ As the railroad was phasing out many of their older two-bay covered hoppers, they needed to be replaced. Frisco turned to Greenville Steel Car for 200 exterior post hoppers constructed between May and June 1977. These 100-ton cars had eight evenly spaced 30-inch hatches with Morton running boards along the centerline of the car roof. The hoppers had center discharge gravity outlets that were painted black, which contrasted nicely with the rest of the body in grey. This order started the use of large sans serif reporting marks and numbers in an UP-like style on covered hoppers. Not surprisingly our sample is in Tulsa, Oklahoma, the major collection point for silica sand covered hoppers on the Frisco, on September 10, 1981. *(Ronald A. Plazzotta)*

78874; series 78750-78974
100-ton LO; 36'11" IL; 2980 cu. ft.

▲ We are fortunate that Ray Kucaba photographed number 78874 with this excellent three-quarter down-on angle in the BN Cicero yard near Chicago on 30th of August 1984. Notice the ex-Frisco high-cube paper car from the 11000 to 11249 series disguised in BN green in the background. The view shows the rooftop details of these cars: the Morton running board; the eight circular 30-inch hatches and their layout; the Ajax hand brake in a low mounted position with the Morton step; and the general welded roof construction. With this group of covered hoppers Frisco purchased kits from Greenville and assembled them at the Springfield shops from April to August 1980. The "BUILT BY FRISCO" stencil is placed below the warning stencil in the middle panel on the side sill angle. Notice the silica sand spilled around the hatches. *(Raymond F. Kucaba)*

Three-Bay Covered Hoppers

SLSF 82359; series 82300-82399
77-ton LO; 41'0" IL; 2893 cu. ft.

▼ It's no surprise that the first three-bay covered hoppers came from Pullman-Standard. The railroad ordered three lots over a span of three years, the first 82000-82199, the second 82200-82299, and the third 82300-82399 from December 1955 to February 1957. They all came equipped with ten unevenly spaced 30-inch loading hatches and six discharge doors and gates from Enterprise. The differences between the lots was the application of the handbrake and running board makes, 82000-82199 series came with Ajax and US Gypsum respectively, while 82200-82399 series came with Miner and Apex Tri-Lok respectively. Our example is found in Alton, Illinois on October 23rd, 1979. *(Raymond F. Kucaba)*

SLSF 182199; series 182000-182399
77-ton LO; 41'0" IL; 2893 cu. ft.
▲ In 1974 the Frisco started to renumber (by adding a"1") and repaint (recondition) at least 100 of the previously mentioned covered hoppers. In the repainting process the bars above and below the reporting marks and numbers were eliminated. These 77-ton cars may have initially been used in grain and feed service but later were mainly used to haul loads of plaster, lime, silica sand, fertilizer, rutile and various chemicals. Looking small amongst 100-ton covered hoppers in Grand Forks, North Dakota on July 25 1983. *(Peter Arnold)*

SLSF 81010; series 81000-81024
100-ton LO; 41'3" IL; 3960 cu. ft.
▼ The ACF Berwick plant built these aluminum-bodied covered hoppers in July 1962. This group was the only one to receive the large coonskin and "Ship it on the Frisco!" slogan painted on natural aluminum. Frisco's first center-outlet covered hopper had six Keystone gravity discharge gates with Wine brand vibrator castings and five 20-inch hatches evenly spaced along the centerline. Number 81024 received gravity-pneumatic outlets. This 100-ton truck sample was rolling through Belt Line Jct. North of Reading, PA on June 25 1976. *(Craig T. Bossler)*

SLSF 85100;
series 85000-85149
100-ton LO; 42'0" IL;
3000 cu. ft.
▶ SL-SF took delivery of 150 covered hoppers from February to May 1964 constructed by Thrall's Chicago Heights, IL plant. Thrall applied ten Standard Railway Equipment Co. roof hatch assemblies and Keystone "Portloc" outlet gates with Wine vibrator fittings. Notice the typical Thrall strengthening angles around the exposed hoppers highlighted in the photo in Denison, Texas on August 26th, 1984. The Frisco mainly hauled cement in these hoppers, observe the cement spill and accumulation around the hatches.
(Richard Yaremko)

SLSF 81409; series 81350-81424
100-ton LO; 49'6" IL; 4427 cu. ft.

▲ Over two separate lots Pullman-Standard built 225 covered hoppers for Frisco. The first lot in April 1964 numbered 81200 to 81349 and this example from the second lot built in January 1965. These were the first covered hoppers to receive trough hatches for quick loading at elevators they also had the largest cubic capacity at the time. Due to the trough on the centerline P-S designed a running board (in this case US Gypsum) that encircled the trough area. This series were fitted with Wine discharge gates and Klasing handbrakes. The railroad served a large area abundant with grain crops and feed mills for poultry and hogs, these were some of the typical loads. Schiller Park, Illinois, June 7 1981. *(Raymond F. Kucaba)*

SLSF 86052; series 86000-86099
100-ton LO; 54'1" IL; 4750 cu. ft.

▼ At the time of purchase these Magor September 1965-built covered hoppers had the largest capacity available. Part of the reason for the increased capacity was the use of aluminum for the body, which reduced the lightweight close to 6,000 pounds compared to the competition P-S 4427 cu. ft. These cars were equipped with trough hatches, Morton running boards, Ellcon-National handbrakes and Wine hopper outlets. For some reason red paint was used for all the lettering, maybe to differentiate them from the steel covered hoppers. Thanks to Dick Kuelbs we are lucky enough to find this rare photo of this car while still clean. Notice the leased USLF P-S 4427cf. covered hopper (mentioned later) next to our sample in Carrollton, Texas on June 28th, 1968. *(Dick*

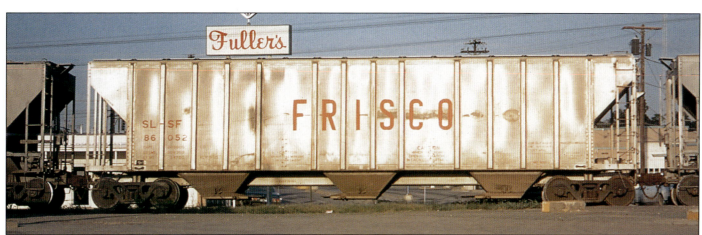

SLSF 79492;
series 79300-79499
100-ton LO; 49'6" IL;
4427 cu. ft.

▶ This group of 200 hoppers came from Pullman-Standard in March 1971, adding to an already 800 strong group purchased and leased in 1967. The 500 leased cars originally carried USLF reporting marks, and then they received SL-SF and were renumbered into the 31000 and later 131000 series. The 1967 Frisco owned 100-ton covered hoppers were numbered in the 79000 to 79299 series. All received gravity outlets of either Wine or Miner types, except for a small group of twenty-three that were equipped with gravity-pneumatic outlets. The 1967's were fitted with Apex running boards and Klasing handbrakes while the 1971's came with Morton and Ellcon equipment respectively. This overhead view in Cicero in September 1985 shows the trough hatches and Morton running boards. *(Raymond F. Kucaba)*

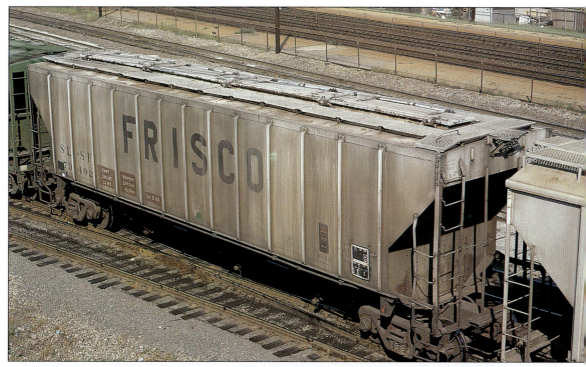

79716; series 79500-79799
100-ton LO; 55'3" IL; 4750 cu. ft.

▲ When Pullman developed a higher capacity covered hopper of 4,750 cubic feet, the Frisco was not far behind, ordering 300 cars in July 1974. This design retained the trough hatch idea although on a "clerestory" roof. Notice that the hoppers are painted black below the side sill and each hopper capacity is stenciled in white. One car from the series, number 79673 received an unusual billboard "FRISCO" in a Futura Black typeface, a black version of the last series of open hoppers built. Caught rolling by in Grand Forks, North Dakota on the 26th of July 1983.

(Peter Arnold)

SLSF 81165; series 79800-79999, 81100-81199
100-ton LO; 55'3" IL; 4750 cu. ft.

▼ Starting with this series of three-bay covered hoppers they received the sans serif UP-like reporting marks and numbers. Pullman-Standard built them between June and July 1977 at their Bessemer, Alabama plant. Morton tread was used for the running boards and steps and also fitted were Ajax hand brakes. The author was able to capture number 81165 in Ferndale, Washington in its intended service on the first of February 1991. *(Nicholas J. Molo)*

SLSF 86793; series 86500-86799
100-ton LO; 55'3" IL; 4750 cu. ft.

▶ Frisco anticipated the merger with the Burlington Northern and specified a green body for the last order of covered hoppers bought by the railroad. With only reporting marks applied it was perhaps rationalized that it was an easy addition to paint a large BN logo on the cars at a later date. These three hundred covered hoppers were delivered by P-S from July to September 1980. Pullman-Standard had revised the shape and size of the jacking pad and pull loop gusset, compare this example with the previous two examples. Here we see an example standing in Saint Paul, Minnesota still very clean and new looking in November 23, 1980. *(Roger Bee)*

Airslide Covered Hoppers

SLSF 81522; series 81508-81522
77-ton LO; 29'6" IL; 2600 cu. ft.

◀ The Frisco's first experience with Airslide covered hoppers was in 1954 when they leased eight 2600 cubic foot cars from General American retaining the GACX reporting marks. Flour was the main commodity hauled in Frisco's airslide hoppers, although perhaps starches and sugars were other loads. Our example group was built in April 1963 while the first group of company owned airslides came in March 1961 (81500-81507). The main design features included six round loading hatches unevenly spaced with two discharge outlets. The cars were fitted with Apex running boards and Equipco handbrakes. Bozo Texino has marked number 81522 in Brookfield, IL on 8 October 1981. Frisco purchased another group of the highly successful 2600 'airslides' in April 1965 (81523-81532).
(Raymond F. Kucaba)

SLSF 81900; series 81900-81910
95-ton LO; 48'11" IL; 4180 cu. ft.

▲ There was a demand for a higher capacity Airslide covered hopper, so in July of 1965 SL-SF received the 4,180 cubic foot version from the GATC East Chicago plant. These cars features ten circular hatches, four discharge gates, and like all Airslide hoppers, had vibrator castings applied to car body sides above the sill. Other identical orders for the 4180 cu. ft. were: 81911-81922 blt. January 1968, 81923-81927 blt. May 1968, 81928-81939 blt. February-March 1969, 81940-81943 blt. May 1969, 81944-81951 blt. January 1970, 81952-81957 blt. September 1972. The class car is shown in Eola, Illinois February 26, 1982. *(Dan Holbrook)*

SLSF 81535; series 81533-81556
77-ton LO; 29'6" IL; 2600 cu. ft.

▲ General American delivered this design phase of single bay covered hoppers in March, April and November 1966. This design differs by the obvious addition of large triangular gussets between the end sheets and the end of car. Other not so obvious design features are full-length side sills and the outer most ribs have changed from C-channels to hat-section ribs. These "airslides" still have high-mounted brake wheels and Apex running boards, but some of the handbrakes were Klasing (like number 81535) and others had Equipco. Dan found our example in West Chicago, IL on March 16 1987. *(Dan Holbrook)*

SLSF 81581; series 81577-81601
77-ton LO; 29'6" IL; 2600 cu. ft.

▼ By the time the last series of single bay Airslide covered hoppers arrived in February 1970, General American designers had made more changes to the design. The elongated dimple has been removed from the gusset, the outer ribs were changed to 4-inch H-columns and the inner ribs had a more C-shape and were broader and harder edged. Also notice the low-mounted Equipco hand brake while sitting in Sherman yard in Texas on September 20, 1981. *(Richard Yaremko)*

Autoracks

**SLSF 3018; series 3001-3090
30-ton FMS; 83'0" IL;**
▲ Frisco was one of the first if not the first railroad to own specially built multi-level automobile carrying flatcars. SL-SF serviced a Chrysler plant on-line in Valley Park, MO, but was also heavily involved in pools with all the other automakers. Pullman-Standard built one prototype tri-level for SL-SF in January 1960, numbered 3000 that included large gussets between the decks and posts. In September Frisco received ninety of this Tri-Dek design (without gussets), which featured extended C-channels above the trucks and P-S 10" travel center-of-car cushioning. Note that the bridge plates were six-foot in length and compatible with themselves and #3000; later cars had TTX-length bridge plates (3091-3130, 3300-3359). Al Holtz was in East St. Louis alongside the TRRA right-of-way on this Saturday September 10, 1960. If you ever wondered how cars were carried on flatcars prior to autoracks, then the car-carrier trailers are shown behind. *(Al Holtz)*

**BTTX 910720; flat class F89eh
72-ton FA; 89'1" IL;
RETURN TO CHEVY PLANT ST. LOUIS, MO**
▼ Check out these shiny Corvettes and one Chevrolet truck! What color do you want? Maybe a convertible! General Motors made Corvettes in Saint Louis (plant closed 1981) from inception till the move to Bowling Green, KY in 1981, seen here close to their birthplace in the TRRA yard in April 1968. The flatcar is built by Pullman-Standard in February 1964 the rack is an early Whitehead & Kales. Note the full-height posts have continuous boltholes, which allows an additional level (tri-level) or able to adjust the rack heights according to specific vehicles. If you look close enough one can make out the adjustable stanchions on the inside of the far side posts (ends connected with cables), they're in the lowest position at the moment. The rack and flat are painted Frisco yellow and the Trailer Train logo and other lettering is in black. *(Emery J. Gulash)*

TTRX 913609; flat class F89fh
72-ton FA; 89'0" IL;
▲ Here is an example of the previously illustrated W&K rack but with an additional level bolted on making it a tri-level. The flatcar was built by Bethlehem Steel Co. in 1964 and carries the then current Trailer Train paint scheme and TTRX reporting marks. Most F89fh class flats received FreightMaster end-of-car cushioning and this example perhaps received the same. The Frisco had an auto-unloading ramp in Irving, Texas where this one is departing north empty in April 1981. *(Tony Lovasz)*

TTBX 961296; flat class BSH10
63.5-ton FA; 89'4" IL;
▼ A colorful assortment of Ford Broncos contrasts with the snow in Whitefish, Montana on December 31, 1984. The Bsh10 class flat was supplied by Bethlehem, while the rack was constructed by Portec-Paragon (note the posts cut flush with the top-deck). From the start Frisco racks were painted yellow and had a large black outline coonskin applied and this look continued till the mid-70's. *(Richard Yaremko)*

TTRX 963026;
flat class BSH11
◀ **52-ton FA; 89'4" IL;**
This fixed deck tri-level has received galvanized corrugated side-panels to protect the loads from vandalism. The Bethlehem built flatcar has a Whitehead & Kales rack welded to the flush-deck. The auto rack is marked NEW 1-70 and carries the typical seventies paint scheme. From this angle at Summit, CA in February 1988 you can make out yellow non-skid paint applied to the deck surfaces as well as a stenciled version of the black coonskin.
(Richard Yaremko)

**TTBX 942083;
flat class PSH20
53.5-ton FA; 89'4" IL;**

◀ Another TTBX bi-level has been captured in Whitefish, MT on December 31, 1984, but this time it has side-panels to protect the vehicles. A separate frame was fabricated to be able to carry the side-panels between and above the levels. This rack has been applied to a Pullman-Standard PSH20 class flatcar built in February 1974. All the top deck trucks are Ford Broncos.
(Richard Yaremko)

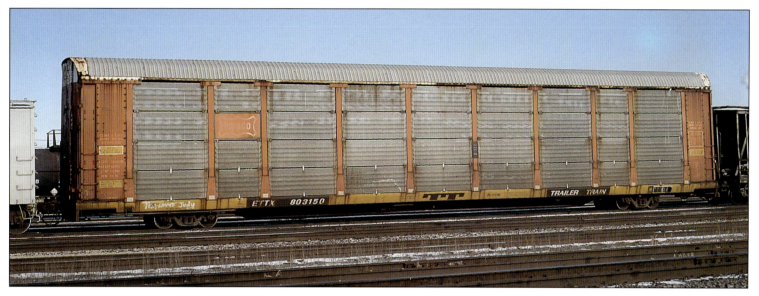

**ETTX 803150 SL-SF R-16; flat class PLH10W
33-ton FA; 89'4" IL;**

▲ In 1969 Frisco lead the way again by being the first railroad to purchase fully enclosed auto racks. By the time 1976 came around Frisco was in need of more auto racks and took delivery of seventy fully-enclosed tri-levels from Portec Inc. in October and November of that year. Ten more tri-level auto racks were added in August 1977. Portec mounted this rack on a Pullman-Standard flatcar class Plh10w ('w' stands for a wide deck flat). These cars came equipped with Youngstown Tri-Fold doors and end-of car cushioning. They were the first series of auto racks that were painted with the Frisco red with a small white outline coonskin on a blank panel. Minneapolis, Minnesota January 24th, 1987. *(Roger Bee)*

**ETTX 820850 SL-SF R 200;
flat class ALH21A
32-ton FA; 89'4" IL;**

◀ SL-SF received another 145 Portec auto racks from January to March 1978 built at their Grand River, Michigan plant. Later in 1979 the Springfield shops were building auto racks from January to May. They utilized flatcars provided by Trailer Train and rack kits from Whitehead & Kales. Unlike the Portec racks these were equipped with clamshell end doors and perhaps ACF FREIGHT-SAVER end-of-car cushioning. Here we see one built in March 1979 on an ACF flat, class ALH21A in Alyth, Alberta on February 22, 1981.
(Richard Yaremko)

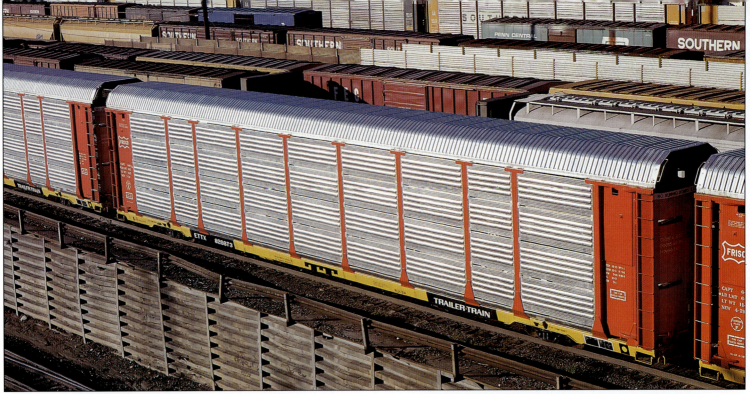

**ETTX 820873 SL-SF R-279; flat class ALH21A
34.5-ton FA; 89'4" IL;**

▲ Can this string of Frisco auto racks get any newer or brighter, as they pass through the Southern yard in Atlanta in May 1979? Atlanta had three auto plants in 1979: General Motors: Doraville (Malibu, Monte Carlo, Cutlass), Lakewood (Grand Prix, Chevette): Ford: Atlanta (Ford LTD). Besides the ETTX reporting marks, the only hint these Frisco assembled W&K racks were tri-levels, were the two cutouts in the end "radial" doors for the decks. The galvanized punched steel panels were produced by Youngstown. Note that one can speculate about the red used on these racks, whereas the use of the small white outline coonskin on the left end panel was consistent. *(Howard L. Robins)*

**ETTX 903916 SL-SF R-334; flat class F89DHW
33.5-ton FA; 89'4" IL;**

▼ The Consolidated Mechanical Shops in Springfield constructed many types of cars and were very skilled to adapt to many variations, this is an example of this point. After the auto rack production was in its last months Trailer Train started to furnish wide body flatcars to the program. This meant that the side posts profile had to change from a jog-in design as the rack joins the flat (see the previous two racks) to a straight down side post like this example. Otherwise these later cars had the same features as the earlier cars, clamshell end doors and end-of-car cushioning. This W&K rack design was assembled in May 1979 and was visiting Los Angeles on 10 March 1985. *(Roger Bee)*

Tractors and Trailers

FRISCO TRANSPORTATION CO., FTC 1650, FCOZ 202002; series FCOZ 202001-202359

▶ Frisco had a subsidiary trucking company appropriately named Frisco Transportation Company that handled less-than-truckload. The original colors for the company were the same as the SLSF locomotives at the time, black and yellow. Here is an example of that yellow and black scheme on a White Diesel in Joplin, Missouri on July 18th 1978. In the background we can make out some trailers back against the platform, one of which is an unknown outside-post trailer with a FCOZ standard TOFC trailer built by Highway. *(Richard Yaremko)*

FRISCO TRANSPORTATION COMPANY, FTC 5, FTC 1649;

◀ When the Frisco changed the locomotive colors to red and white FTC followed suit. A White truck in Joplin wears the attractive red and white scheme on a July day in 1978. This shot also demonstrates the tri-wing FTC logo clearly on both trailers one has been riveted on a sheet panel while the other is a sticker placed directly on the metal panels. *(Richard Yaremko)*

FTC 1608;
Z; 40'0" OL

▶ On a perfectly clear and sunny September 20, 1981, Richard Yaremko snapped number FTC 1608 in Sherman, Texas. The builder of this trailer is Dorsey, constructed with aluminum outside sheathing. Note the solid wheels used for the fifth-wheel. *(Richard Yaremko)*

FCOZ 500026;
series 500001-500030
Z; 40'0" OL;
Refrigerator; 1995 cu. ft.

◀ Roger Bee captured this insulated trailer a bit the worse for wear in Rochester, Minnesota in 1997. Trailmobile built this group of thirty reefers in the early-60's; besides the builder's logo the oversized fifth-wheel gusset is a spotting feature. Originally there was a Transicold Model 250C refrigeration unit with a 110-gallon diesel tank under slung between the fifth wheel and the tandem tires. These trailers wore the "Ship it on the Frisco!" slogan with the front-end white coonskin within a red rectangle; other trailers used a black rectangle behind the white coonskin. *(Roger Bee)*

**XFCZ 970145;
series 970102-970201
Z; 40'0" OL;
Drop-deck; 3030 cu. ft.**

◀ Frisco leased these drop-frame trailers from Xtra Inc. This type of trailer was popular with southeastern railroads for hauling furniture and carpets for example. The overall height of this trailer is 13-feet six-inches. Dorsey is the builder of this trailer pictured in Sarcee, Alberta on July 5th 1981. The 'FC' in 'XFCZ' was the abbreviation that Xtra used for Frisco leased trailers. The other major leasing company, REALCO, used 'RFCZ' reporting marks. The coonskin decal on the front-end came in red and black background versions.
(Richard Yaremko)

**XFCZ 297407;
series 297400-297499
Z; 40'0" OL; Dry-van;
2750 cu. ft.**

▶ Another Dorsey built van, this time constructed with fiberglass-reinforced plywood side panels, FRP for short. This was an attempt to reduce the overall lightweight of the trailer without sacrificing the sidewall strength. Frisco joined other railroad piggyback service advertising and came up with their own "piggy" caricature and slogan "PIGS ARE BEAUTIFUL". Craig Walker was lucky enough to find this piggy on the Santa Fe in San Bernardino, CA on March the 15th 1980. *(Craig Walker)*

**FCOZ 202234, 202102;
series 202001-202359
Z; 40'0" OL; Dry-van;
2740 cu. ft.**

◀ Here are two examples of dry-van trailers built by Highway, found in Tennessee yard near Memphis on September 22, 1980. Both have had the "PIGS ARE BEAUTIFUL" logo, ACI label and red and yellow "CAUTION HIGH TRAILER 13FT. 6IN." decals applied. Not all FCOZ reporting marks and numbers were black, at least number 202234 is in red.
(Nicholas J. Molo collection)

Non-Revenue Equipment

Wrecking Cranes and Equipment

SLSF 99030; series 99030-99034
100-ton; MWW; Steam Wrecking Crane

◄ In 1955 this 100-ton steam wrecking crane was assigned Sherman, Texas. In this photo on the tracks behind the Springfield shops number 99030 is looking serviceable on May 16th 1970. This crane was built by Industrial Works in 1909 and has a boom swing of 25-feet. *(Owen Leander)*

SLSF 99021 Tulsa, 109319; series 99021, 99022, 99025, 109000-109702
250-ton MWW; Diesel Wrecking Crane; 55-ton MW; 42'6" IL; Boom Flat Car

▼ Frisco ordered this wrecking crane from Industrial Brownhoist in February 1954 and assigned it to Tulsa. Two other identical 250-ton wreckers were 99022 and 99025, assigned to Springfield and Memphis. They were all diesel powered and had a 50-foot boom swing radius. A matching silver-grey painted boom car came from a flatcar series originally built during 1951 to 1954 by ACF. Captured in its assigned yard Tulsa, on October 3rd 1977.

(Richard Yaremko)

SLSF 99071 (DL-919), 100114; series 99036 99072, 100000-100142
MWS; Diesel Wrecking Crane: 55-ton MW; 42'6" IL; Boom Flat Car

▲ A turnout has been placed on the coupled flatcar, still in its revenue service yellow although renumbered for M of W service. The flatcar was constructed by ACF in February 1954, original car series 95900 to 95999. This diesel-electric crane built by American Hoist & Derrick was self-propelled. The photographer snapped number 99071 on the 4th of October 1977 in Tulsa.

(Richard Yaremko)

SLSF RL-038; Diesel Crane
◀ Photographed in Baxter Springs, Kansas, on the 14th of August 1977. This Frisco Burro crane is a Model 40 and able to handle 12.5-tons. They were also able to move under their own power. The two red Frisco coonskin decals make this plain yellow crane into a classy scheme. They are very useful multi-purpose lightweight cranes that could be used on small roadway projects like track work, tie replacements and bridgework. *(Richard Yaremko)*

SLSF 109515;
series 109000-109702
77-ton MW; 65'6" IL;
1777 cu. ft.
▼ A few revenue gondolas were demoted to company service duties, including this sixty-five foot example. It probably came from a group of gons built in 1948 by Pressed Steel Car Co. (70000 to 70049). Its company service duties on this day in July 1984 were as a boom tender, found in Pleasanton, KS.
(Tony Lovasz)

SLSF 104403;
series 104401-104419
50-ton MW; 40'7" IL;
ASSIGNED TO M. OF W. ROADWAY MACHINE WK. EQUIPT.
◀ Well into 1985 and this boom car sits near the Irving, Texas depot in a work train. The flatcar has its origins in 1928 when it was built by GATC. A bit less than half of the car is occupied with a steel-framed wood-sheathed shelter that at one time may have contained spare parts for cranes.
(Tony Lovasz)

Work Gang Cars

**SLSF 102916;
MW; 71'9" IL; KITCHEN
& DINER OFFICE
& BUNK**

◀ This probably is an ex-coach built by ACF in 1926, lot number 98, then rebuilt by SLSF in the 1930s or 1940s. Sometime in the '60's when the demand for passenger cars diminished this car was converted to the stenciled service. The rooftop vents were a telltale sign where the kitchen was located in the ex-coach. Observe the window air-conditioning frame jutting from one of the central windows. Waiting for its next call to duty in Memphis, Tennessee on April 6, 1984.
(Charles H. Zeiler)

**SLSF 105397;
MW; 81'11" IL; M. OF W.
STEEL BRIDGE GANG
KITCHEN & DINER
& BUNK**

▶ The Springfield shops converted this ex-sleeper in 1956 and repainted it in April 1960. Its original assignment was Steel Bridge Gang #902 and perhaps has remained in that service on this May 1970 day in Kansas City. The sleeper has been retrofitted with cooking facilities note the extra venting stacks coming from the roof and vent holes to the outside.
(Owen Leander)

115

**SLSF 109121;
MW; 66'0" IL;
TOOL CAR**

◀ This Tool Car was once a baggage car, perhaps built by ACF in 1912 and probably ex-370-380. It was repaired and repainted in Fort Worth for its current service in September 1968. Painted in the typical maintenance of way silver-grey in Irving, TX, February 8th 1983.
(Lynn Savage)

Ballast and Air Dump Cars

**SLSF 96500; series 96500-96552
77-ton HT; 32'8" IL; 2075 cu. ft.**

▶Two hundred cars were originally built between May and November 1946 by American Car & Foundry. These had an offset hopper style top chord detail. Then in 1962 Springfield undertook a rebuilding program to repair these ballast hoppers (the offset was welded over), they were numbered in the 96100-96299 series. In 1974 Frisco needed to recondition some of these hoppers once again, while others were scrapped. Part of the reconditioning program involved welding a top channel to the top chord to strengthen the car sides. Ajax handbrakes and Enterprise discharge gates were originally fitted. Here is an example of one of these second rebuilds at Baxter Springs in Kansas on August 14, 1977.
(Richard Yaremko)

**SLSF 97024;
series 97000-97039
90-ton MWB;
38'0" IL; 2400 cu. ft.**

◀ Not until June 1971 did Frisco received forty new ballast hoppers from Thrall Car Company. Notice the all-welded side posts and C-channel end posts with rivets. A unique feature of these cars was that the corner end ladder combination tilted inward at the top two rungs. The door opening mechanism and draft gear were Miner products and the handbrakes from Universal. This low Texas sunset highlights the details in Irving on a day in February 1984. The Frisco used Chat as their ballast of choice for the most part. Chat is tailings from mining operations and is off-white to light grey color.
(Tony Lovasz)

**SLSF 97048; series 97040-97089
90-ton MWB; 38'0" IL;
2400 cu. ft.**

▶The Frisco was sufficiently impressed with the Thrall design and opted to purchase fifty kits and assemble them at their Springfield shops. The new ballast hoppers rolled out of the shops between August and December 1975. The only difference from the earlier cars was in the paint scheme applied, the addition of the white large sans serif "FRISCO", and the replacement of the Thrall builder's logo with a "BUILT BY FRISCO" logo. The car is fitted with Ajax hand brakes and Enterprise discharge gates allowing the ballast to be placed almost anywhere across the track profile. South Superior, Wisconsin 15 July 1987. (Roger Bee)

**SLSF 103032;
series 103029-103038
93-ton MWD; 38'9" IL;
1350 cu. ft.**

▶ Frisco management had ordered three previous groups of air dump cars from Magor in 1954, and Difco in 1971 and 1974. Following these was and order for ten air dump gons from PACCAR in April 1978. From this side you can easily make out the oversized dumping air reservoir and air cylinders. These dump cars were used to unload riprap and aggregates to the sides of the right of way. Here we see number 103032 in Allouez, WI on July 19th 1998. *(Roger Bee)*

**SLSF 97126; series 97100-97164
100-ton HT; 32'8" IL; 2180 cu. ft.**

▲ As late as December 1979 to March 1980 Bethlehem Steel Co. delivered 65 ballast hoppers. These again were of a different design with two pairs of discharge chutes and fully riveted side posts. The lettering diagram specified the same but small version typeface of the large "FRISCO" for the reporting marks and numbers. Also the oversized "MWB" left no doubt the assignment of this car, maintenance of way ballast. A sample from this series is found in South Superior, Wisconsin on July 15, 1987. *(Roger Bee)*

**SLSF 103041; series 103039-103048
73.5-ton MWD; 41'9" IL; 1350 cu. ft.**

▼ Chuck Zeiler was able to capture Difco's version of their air dump car on the last day of 1987 in Cicero yard. Difco constructed these 10 cars between June and December 1980. Even though the cubic capacity was the same as the PACCAR version, it (Difco) was achieved with three-feet greater in length and lower side gates. *(Charles H. Zeiler)*

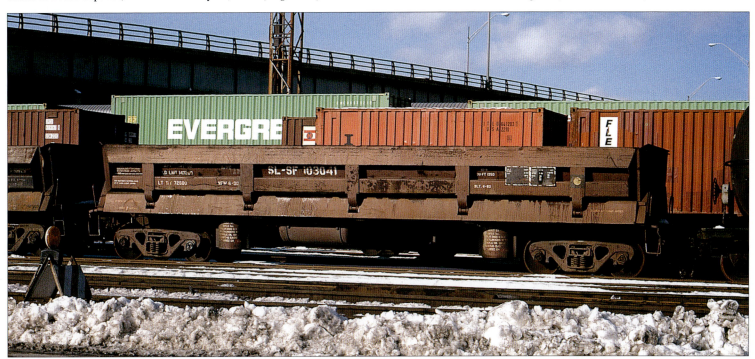

Miscellaneous Equipment

SLSF RC-2169; Speeder
◄ This immaculate Fairmont speeder sits gleaming on a clear day in May 1971 in Stroud, Oklahoma. The cast nose and handles have been polished along with the chromed mudguards. These contrast well with yellow body, black wheels and window gaskets and set-off with a perfectly positioned red Frisco coonskin sticker. Stroud is located on the mainline between Tulsa and Oklahoma City. The agent stands in the background outside the typical seventies beige and white Frisco depot "shed", along with train order signals and order stand. *(Emery J. Gulash)*

SLSF IJ-914; Ballast Regulator
► This ballast regulator sits idle on industrial track just to the east of the Irving depot on the 7th of February 1976. Most if not all Frisco track equipment received yellow paint finished with a small red coonskin sticker. This regulator was built by Tamper a MK II Electromatic model that used an alignment buggy (in silver-gray) for laser alignment.
(Tony Lovasz)

SLSF 99101; series 99101-99102; Spreader
◄ The numbering is a bit confusing, it seems the 99101 was number 99100 (although Frisco records had two in the series), but it is sub-numbered JD-003 suggesting there are at least three of these Jordan spreaders. Frisco used their spreaders mainly for ballast control therefore the low blade profile. Number 99101 is coupled to an ex-Frisco GP38-2 in Irving, Texas in August 1984.
(Tony Lovasz)

SLSF 99157; series 99156-99161; Scale Test Car

▶ The Saint Louis–San Francisco Railway had at least a couple types of scale test cars; this is one example in Memphis, Tennessee in June 1973. The Southwark-Baldwin Corporation built number 99157 in June 1941. The carbody was of all cast steel construction and had a portal to add or subtract weights. The other Frisco known type of scale test car was built by Maxson, to an all-welded design on standard two axle trucks. *(Bernie Wooller)*

SLSF 104042; series 104000-104091 50-ton MWF; 38'3" IL; 2620 cu. ft.

◀ In 1980 CMS Springfield shops converted at least 64 wood racks and bulkhead flats into chain tie cars from different heritage. Most of which used the 1952 Frisco built (from GSC kits) 38-foot 3-inch IL wood racks, others utilized a variety of 49-foot 1-inch wood racks or 48-foot 6-inch bulkhead flats. The conversion involved applying a curtain of chain lengths to the sides for easy removal by crews. This very clean (most were covered with creosote) example is seen in Tulsa, Oklahoma on the 6th of November 1981. *(Ronald A. Plazzotta)*

SLSF 104368; series 104352-104381 77-ton MW; 29'3" IL; 1958 cu. ft.

▶ In 1969 Frisco re-assigned several ex-covered hoppers into Diesel Sand hopper service. Most of the covered hoppers used were taken from the August 1948 built by Mount Vernon Car Co. Although research has found one example of one stenciled for April 1942 (#104379), but that may have been incorrectly stenciled. Their were three distinct paint schemes applied to these cars: all-black body with white reporting marks; original grey with large black "FRISCO" with over-painted numbers (our example); and a total repaint in silver-grey with a 24-inch black outline coonskin. In a typical setting for these covered hoppers sitting next the Lindenwood yard (St. Louis) sanding tracks in March 30th, 1982. *(Ronald A. Plazzotta)*

**SLSF 104608; series 104600-104679
55-ton MWF; 40'7" IL;**

▲ Almost 100 flatcars from the 95300 to 95799 group built by General American Tank Co. in 1928 were demoted to maintenance of way service. Our example built in September of 1928 still carried the original Frisco oxide red paint and is in ribbon rail service. The patches of paint and newer stencils tell us some of the history this car has been through. Dan Holbrook captures this 54-year old survivor near home at the BN Eola yard in October 1982.

**SLSF 109335;
series 109000-109702
55-ton MWF; 42'6" IL;**

▶ This group of cars included demoted boxcars, gondolas and flatcars for maintenance of way service. Here we see a 1951 ACF built flatcar in yellow loaded with two reconditioned switcher trucks chained to rails. This viewing angle allows us to make out the end details of a drop shaft Superior handbrake and AAR standard type 'E' coupler. Saint Louis, Missouri December 18th 1982. *(Charles H. Zeiler)*

**SLSF 191077;
series 191000-191129
55-ton MW; 37'2" OL;
10,213 gals.**

◀ Number 191077 was in Wichita, Kansas on a sunny day in July 1982. ACF delivered one hundred and thirty 10,213-gallon tank cars from its Milton plant between July and November 1949. These welded tank cars arrived painted black with a yellow dome and assigned as stenciled for "DIESEL FUEL LOADING ONLY". Burlington Northern continued to utilize these tank cars in their intended service and collection of waste oil.

(Tony Lovasz)

SLSF 101166; NE; 29'2" IL;
▲ A handful of cabooses received silver paint for maintenance of way service and some were renumbered like number 101166. Notice how the yellow handrails and ladders compliment the unique yellow background black outlined coonskin. The exact origin is unknown but it seems its heritage is SLSF built from 1938 to 1946 that has been re-sheathed with plywood panels. Howard Robins found our example in Memphis, TN in June 1973. *(Howard L. Robins)*

***Herman* and (unknown) with *Blakely*; Tug Boats and Barges**
▼ One of the unique operations on the Frisco (ex-Alabama, Tennessee & Northern) was rail barge service to Blakely Island on the east side of the Port of Mobile, Alabama. SL-SF owned two barges for the operation (although one was used at any one time), while the tugboats (usually in pairs) were contracted. The industries served on the island included chemical and petroleum processors, scrap yards and shipbuilding. The cars on *Blakely* today the 19th of August 1968 reflect the loads and empties needed for these industries. On the Blakely Island side the Frisco had a 45-ton GE switcher and later a SW-1 stationed there for switching duties. Both operations usually had one to two SL-SF idler flats to shove the cars on the barges. *(Nicholas J. Molo collection)*

Cabooses

SLSF 14; series 10-26; NE; 29'2" IL;

▶ Howard Robins was on hand in May of 1966 to take this classic shot of the conductor climbing his caboose near the depot in Bessemer, Alabama. The number 14 was the assigned caboose at the time for the Bessemer road-switcher job originating from the East Thomas yard near Birmingham, Alabama. These cabooses were built in 1938 by the Frisco shops and had a steel underframe, carbody frame and cupola. The sides were sheathed with wood and painted the standard "Freight Car Red #116" and a black background coonskin with a small "Ship it on the Frisco!" slogan. The combination of the aforementioned details and Frisco great proportions for equipment make this a very attractive transition period caboose. *(Howard L. Robins)*

SLSF 119; series 100-119; NE; 29'2" IL;

▲ Frisco built these twenty cabooses in October and November 1946. The design closely followed previous homebuilt cabooses with the addition of a heating oil fill near the cupola clearly seen here. The roof seems to have retained the original mule hide with batten combination. The steel cupola sits on a steel frame body and underframe and sheathed with wood. The SL-SF shops forged and stamped the wheel and staff handbrakes and brake levers and rigging. This action shot taken from the Ewing Street footbridge in Saint Louis in February 1963 allows us to witness a vigilant crew in the cupola on a transfer run back to Lindenwood yard. What's special about his scene is the period boxcars in the background, including Frisco or Katy and UP passenger equipment further back in the Jefferson Avenue coach yard. *(Paul C. Winters)*

SLSF 1140; series 1112-1199; NE; 29'2" IL;

▼ By the time the seventies came the 1946 built cabooses needed updating and repair. The reconditioning included the replacement of the wood sheathing with plywood, galvanized roof sheets and the removable of the wooden running boards and end ladders. After shopping they were renumbered into the 1100 series and received a new paint job. These cabooses were still very useful for the railroad in demoted service like locals, road switcher jobs and transfer jobs. Bill Phillips captured number 1140 in Fort Worth on a sunny March 14 1976 probably in transfer service. *(Bill Phillips, Roger Bee collection)*

SLSF 163;

▶ In early 1964 SL-SF purchased the North East Oklahoma Railroad, besides the right of way and Alco switchers came a group of cabooses. Here is an example of one of the four cabooses, which the NEO built at their Miami, Oklahoma shops between 1947 and 1951 (our example was built in May 1951). Like the Alco switchers the Frisco kept the centered cupola NEO built caboose in home territory and here we see number 163 in Miami, OK on March 16, 1967. At least two had been renumbered into the 1100 series, although photos reveal numbers 1110, 1111, 1162 and 1163 were used. *(Roger Bee collection)*

SLSF 1184;
series 1184; NE; 29'2" IL;

▲ In 1971 Frisco selected a 1952 homebuilt caboose numbered 154 to become a test bed to apply bay-windows to these cabooses. Number 1184 is a result of the rebuilding that included the removal of the cupola, end ladders and running boards, re-roofing, rebuilding of the end steps, the addition of plywood sides and aluminum-framed windows. Notice the bank of batteries hung below the bay for the radio equipment. Unique yellow bay stripes set this caboose from the typical, coupled in the East Thomas yard in Birmingham on the end of a transfer job.
(Nicholas J. Molo collection)

SLSF 213; series 200-274; NE; 30'1" IL;

▲ In another first for the Frisco, they were the first major railroad to buy into the "WIDE-VISION" cupola idea. They purchased 75 cabooses for mainline service built by the International Railway Car Company between February and May 1957 at their Kenton, Ohio plant. This group was renumbered into the 1200 series in 1968 to avoid locomotive number conflicts when the Frisco installed a system computer. They came equipped with all the latest modern conveniences for crews, Waugh 10-inch travel cushioned underframes, Duo-Therm space heater with Brighton-Dickson smoke jack, Marquette water cooler and radio powered by batteries charged by an electric generator belt driven to the axles. The original freight car red paint scheme is still intact in this photo taken in October 1960 in Oklahoma City. Note the black stripe the full length on the "ZU" plate and around the cupola sides. Other details worth mentioning are the Pyle-National midget marker lamps with shields welded to the body, and the trust plate above those, Bendix-King antenna on the cupola roof and Ajax non-spin handbrake.

(K. B. King Jr., Daniel Kohlberg collection)

SLSF 1214; series 1200-1274; NE; 30'1" IL;

▲ Howard Robins was on-hand in Birmingham, Alabama to capture number 1214 at the tail of an incoming train in May 1974. By this date the 1957-built caboose has been renumbered and also has been repainted into a caboose red but lacks the "SOUTHEAST…SOUTHWEST" slogan on the cupola side. The Frisco shops performed some minor alterations at the same time like replacing the Bendix-King antenna with a whip type, the electric marker lamps were moved to the cupola roof and some of the brake wheels were replaced with a forged type. This view is a great vantage point to notice other parts applied by ICC: toilet vent, Apex "Tri-Lok" running boards, end platforms and steps with nose checker plate, and 10" Waugh cushioning. *(Howard L. Robins)*

SLSF 1240; series 1200-1274; NE; 30'1" IL;

▼ Frisco got into the spirit of the Bi-centennial celebrations by painting a handful of cabooses into two special schemes. The more common of the two is shown here in Mobile, Alabama in June 1975 all dressed in red, white and blue. This photo allows us a good look at the outside swinghanger-equalized GSC trucks characteristic to this group of caboose. Also the electric generator before the right-hand truck and typical Frisco-style battery box can be seen clearly. All of the railings, brake wheels, ladder and step stiles received white paint, whereas the air-line shut-off valve was painted red along with the cupola. The non-overhanging body and cupola roofs of this series have been painted with non-skid black car cement. *(Howard L. Robins)*

SLSF 1275; series 1275-1284; NE; 30'1" IL;

◀ In June 1968 Frisco ordered another ten cabooses from International Car Co. and delivered in the caboose red scheme. It was over ten years since SL-SF purchased new cabooses from ICC and a lot of details had changed since the first order. The overall dimensions remained the same including the window arrangement for the body and the cupola. However, the changes involved the use of an overhanging Stanray roof, Apex running board, steps and platforms, S.C.T. Co. trucks, non-spin Ellcon handbrakes, a different smoke jack and vents, Caban heater, and smaller battery box. By this August 17 day in 1980 the paint scheme matches the locomotives photographed in Fort Worth, Texas. Another key feature changed during the application of the new paint, was the replacement of the cupola roof markers to a position on the roof end sheets, notice the electrical conduit from the original position. Again the underframe was cushioned with a 10-inch travel Waugh type.
(Bill Phillips, Roger Bee collection)

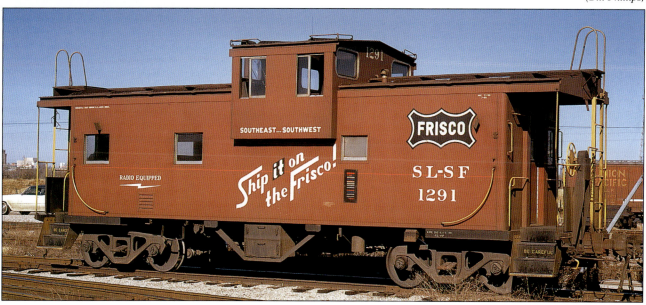

SLSF 1291; series 1285-1292; NE; 30'1" IL;

▲ The following year, 1969, Frisco received another eight cabooses from ICC in July and August. International Car by this date had changed the cupola to a lower clearance plate and therefore looks squatter on the body. This caboose with an almost pristine paint scheme has the "SOUTHEAST...SOUTHWEST" slogan on the cupola was captured in Oklahoma City on 11 December 1971. The overhanging roof has a black cement non-skid finish accounting for the difference in color from the PPG red caboose paint. The small window to the right of the cupola was the toilet window, which was common to all the Frisco ICC cabooses. Like the previous order the running boards and end platforms were Apex, the three steps were Apex with checker plate nosing. The handbrakes again were Ellcon mounted on angular formed stanchions. Like the other ICC cabooses these came equipped with radios, this series had whip antennas with Motorola radios. *(Owen Leander)*

SLSF 1180; series 1100-1195; NE; 29'2" IL;

▶ Around the late sixties the railroad purchased surplus Santa Fe cabooses to supplement their dwindling stock of cabooses for locals. They lacked radios, cushioning and running boards, but they received a new coat of paint and the Frisco coonskins and some like this one received the "Ship it on the Frisco!" slogan. They were numbered and mixed throughout the same series as the Frisco built cupola cabooses. Richard Yaremko snapped number 1180 on the end of its train in Tulsa, Oklahoma on October 16th 1976.
(Richard Yaremko)

SLSF 1311, 1326, 1339; series 1300-1343; NE; 7'9" IL;

▲▲▼ The Frisco had the need for terminal cabooses due to its many switch jobs and transfer drags in major cities like St. Louis, Kansas City, Memphis, Tulsa, Birmingham, and Ft. Smith and Springfield. Starting in 1967 the Springfield shops converted three 40' 7" flatcars built in 1928 by General American in the 95300-95799 series into transfer cabooses. Later in 1968 they converted another forty from 42' 6" flatcars built in 1951 and 1954 by ACF in the 95800-95999 series. Typically most of the terminal cabooses were painted in a couple versions of caboose red (a brighter version in later years) and at least one was painted yellow, number 1306 later number 1326 as demonstrated here in Pensacola, Florida in August 1978. The red cars used either black background or just white outline coonskins. Number 1326 shows the oil tank mounted on the deck for the heater within the "doghouse"; this square tank was the most typical however 40-gallon drums were used as well. The West Springfield shops retained the flatcar ASF coil-spring trucks, while fabricating the doghouse on flatcar, the stanchions, railings and brake stand. Number 1311 like some others had an addition of two large riveted gussets on each side connecting the doghouse to the flatcar. Company officials look on at 1311 in Memphis on a day in June 1973, note the assignment stenciled in white on the doghouse. The K C Terminal was assigned number 1339, seen in one of the KC yards at the end of its train on May 3rd 1970. The shops would use whatever they had on hand for brake wheels, as can be seen in these examples. *(Howard L. Robins) (Nicholas J. Molo collection) (Owen Leander)*

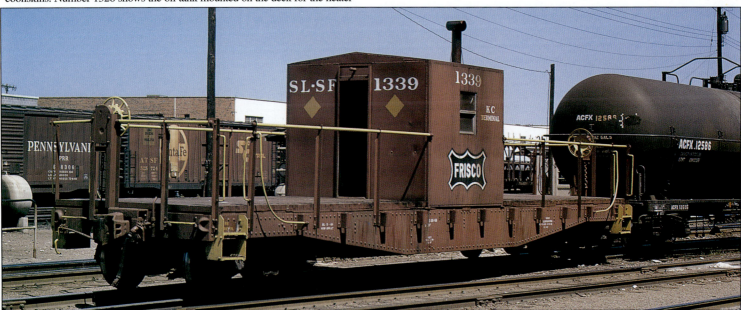

SLSF 1776; series 1776; NE; 29'9" IL;

▲ You'd be hard pressed to find a better looking Bi-centennial caboose anywhere, complete with seal, a star for each of the original 13 states and fifty stars on the flag. This was a homebuilt caboose constructed in May of 1972, the first of many similar cabooses built at the Consolidated Mechanical Shops. Frisco utilized excess forty-foot PS-1 boxcars as fodder for the caboose program, while the cupolas were fabricated into an ICC-like design. Number 1776 is unique compared to the others being ten-inches longer, has P-S roof panels over the body and cupola, larger side windows (although identically positioned), and detail differences in the battery box. The left truck has an axle generator attached to keep the batteries charged for the radio and other electrical appliances. Due to the crews liking of the cushioning on the 1200 series cabooses, these were also fitted with cushioning. K.B. King recorded this caboose in Fort Worth in 1974.

(K. B. King Jr., Daniel Kohlberg collection)

SLSF 1704; series 1700-1725; NE; 29'9" IL;

▼ The forty-foot boxcar to caboose conversion program started in earnest in February 1973 with the completion of class cabooses numbered 1700 and 1400. The 1700 series were intended for pooled road service, which included radios and cushioning. Whereas, the 1400 series cabooses would be assigned to locals that didn't require radios and cushioning, although the crews would argue that point. Here we see a typical example of the rebuilding in Wichita, Kansas on July 29th of 1977. The remainder of the 1700's were steadily converted from March 1973 till November 1974. Many features of the boxcars are evident on the cabooses; they retained most of the welded side panels and side sill profile, P-S roof panels (although when needed these would be replaced like on this example) and some kept the dimples in the roof end sheets. This cupola clearly shows the typical smooth welded roof sheets and the red paint scheme originally applied.

(Peter Arnold)

SLSF 1724; series 1700-1725; NE; 29'9" IL;

▶ This example demonstrates the mandarin red and white paint scheme in Saint Louis on April 16th, 1977. Notice how the side windows differ from 1776's in being more rectangular. The roof of the cupola are home to the Frisco-style twin Pyle-National midget marker lamps and whip-type antenna. This excellent shot also allows a closer look at the end steps, platform end sill, brake stand and other end details (they all lacked running boards). This typical battery box had a flip down top half door, which allowed access to the terminals.

(Ronald A. Plazzotta)

SLSF 1434; series 1400-1442; NE; 29'9" IL;
▲ Here is an example of a 1400 series caboose at the tail end of its train in Tulsa, Oklahoma on August 26, 1980, probably a local in its intended service. That's why this caboose lacks the "RADIO EQUIPPED" lettering with lightning bolt, the antenna and cushioned underframe. These forty-three cabooses were converted from February 1973 until October 1976; again the system shops in Springfield, Missouri performed the work. Number 1434 shows us the other side of the caboose, which has only two aluminum-framed side windows and common to the 1700's as well. Other details to be aware of is the addition of a rain gutter above the cupola side windows and the lack of P-S dimples on the roof end sheets, which has a single red marker lamp attached. *(Roger Bee)*

**SLSF 1727, 1732;
series 1726-1735; NE; 29'9" IL;**
◄ ▲ In November and December 1979 the Springfield shops were at it again and produced the last ten cabooses for the railroad. Unusual for the Frisco these were of the "bay-window" design and had a strong resemblance to contemporary bay-window offerings. The X-panel Stanray roof and smoke jack position is clearly seen in the shot of number 1727 in Irving, Texas on a sunny day in December 1979. It's noticeable in the photo that the bay window is actually offset to one end and there are two evenly sized and spaced windows this side of the caboose. Whereas, the other side of the caboose the right-side window is a smaller fixed and frosted toilet window. The radio whip-type antenna is visible fixed upon a small elevated box welded on the roof. The battery box has been located very close to the successful axle generator from the 1700 and 1400 series cabooses. Instead of a cushioned underframe these cars had end-of-car cushioning, plainly seen springs are mounted below the coupler. The paint diagram had a slight variation due to the bay-window placement, a white-outlined coonskin was placed in the red band below the windows. The "BUILT BY FRISCO" inside the small coonskin on the side sill shows up well in the shot of number 1732 in Memphis on a cloudless sky in January 1981. *(Tony Lovasz, Roger Bee collection)*